UNRAVEL YOU

An Authentic Guide to Self-Reflection
and Self-Discovery for
Moms Who Want More from Life

Praise for *Unravel You*

In *Unravel You*, Adrienne Giffen has given the world a precious gift: the gift of her own personal story and path through adversity to self-knowledge, to self-acceptance and ultimately to living a life of true, authentic fulfillment and joy. And with the brilliant journaling questions and prompts in the end of each chapter, she gives readers an experiential blueprint to know themselves on a deeper level and potentially achieve the same fulfillment.

Adrienne learned to trust her inner voice, to find a life rich with lessons learned. Now that voice is a guiding light and beacon of inspiration and encouragement. *Unravel You* is a self-help marvel with a splash of memoir to take one on an exciting journey of self-discovery. I highly recommend it!

The fun companion *Now You're Talking*™ board game brings the same sense of valuable self-exploration to a memorable and entertaining experience for the whole family!

~ *Laura Robinson*
Emmy-nominated Television Executive Producer
Co-author of *Chicken Soup for the Soul's* book,
Count Your Blessings
Co-inventor of *Balderdash*, board game

Unravel You is a gift. By sharing her most painful and joyful experiences, Adrienne Giffen gives us a road map to a values-aligned life. Affirming and challenging, this book sets the wheels in motion to a more authentic you!

~ Adine Mees

The author's presentation of her personal experiences within a theoretical and interactive context makes for compelling reading.

~ Laurel Kurtenbach

You will want to read how Adrienne masterfully evokes discovery and self-reflection to understand the path you are on and where you are going.

~ Nancy Hazelwood

Adrienne asks the reader questions throughout her book that made me stop and think about adversity in my life, my heartaches, my wins, my loves, and what contributed to the fabric of my life. Since reading *Unravel You*, I have been paying more attention to what truly makes me dance, and I have started putting myself first from time to time.

~ Jana Koldova

Grab your magic markers and get ready to stop and think. Adrienne has created a captivating guide to help structure and understand thoughts and feelings that otherwise I would have missed or struggled to gather. This book has given me an opportunity to explore and better understand who I strive to be. I look forward to revisiting these exercises as I grow.

~ Fay Egan

Adrienne's book reminds me how blessed I really am. There have been some hard times for sure, but you'll usually find me on the dance floor. Thanks for the reminder.

~ Robyn Kitchen

Through vulnerably sharing stories of the extraordinary highs and lows from her own life and reflecting on what each experience revealed about the truth of who she is, Adrienne lights the way for us to examine our past experiences. Through powerful questions, Adrienne encourages us to reflect on our own journey and find the hidden truths buried in our stories that provide the clues to who we truly are.

~ Caroline Grubb

UNRAVEL YOU

YOU

An Authentic Guide to Self-Reflection
and Self-Discovery for
Moms Who Want More from Life

ADRIENNE GIFFEN

Seshat Press
211 Pauline Drive #513
York, PA 17402
www.seshatpress.com
Send questions to: support@seshatpress.com

Paperback ISBN: 979-8-9915156-8-9
eBook ISBN: 979-8-9915156-9-6
Library of Congress Control Number: 2024925119

Cover Design: Ranilo Cabo
Layout: Ranilo Cabo
Editor and Proofreader: Heather Taylor
Book Midwife: Karen Everitt

Printed in the United States of America

Seshat Press is proud to be a part of the Tree Neutral® program. Tree Neutral offsets the number of trees consumed in the production and printing of this book by taking proactive steps such as planting trees in direct proportion to the number of trees used to print books. To learn more about Tree Neutral, please visit treeneutral.com.

To Beau, for your love, your encouragement, and your laughter. Thank you for knowing me and loving me anyway. You make me dance.

Contents

Foreword

It can be hard to be a person.

If you're as lucky as I have been to grow up in an industrialized nation as a person with a degree of privilege, you might ask yourself if it's really *that* hard, given the numerous ways in which we have been blessed. But the human experience has its hardships at every level, and life is not a journey of comparisons. Or it shouldn't be, anyway. Where's the value in that?

Turning over the moments of our lives in our minds, as Adrienne does as she takes you through her story, is one of the many ways we find the value we're looking for in our own existence.

Years ago, my mother shared with me a quote attributed to Socrates: *The unexamined life is not worth living.* I asked if that meant we were supposed to examine every outcome before we took a step—I didn't love that idea.

But, no, she told me, the examination of life isn't a stop sign; it is about reflection. It's a process that allows us to take the time to look backward, consider our journey and all its learnings, and then apply these as we move forward to build a life worth living. All good experiments include starting with hypotheses, moving through experimentation, and then reviewing to determine what we have, in fact, learned.

The journey you're about to embark on with Adrienne is one that will take you through her story, demonstrating the experiments she has engaged in and how she has reflected on these to create learnings that she has applied to live the life she does today. The tools she has picked up along the way are scattered throughout the chapters of this book, so you can try them out as she draws you toward creating your unique hypotheses, experiments, and learnings.

Adrienne, like you, was made for joy. Like all of us, she's been created to dance. Sometimes those dances are easy, reflexive, and smooth. Sometimes those dances require practice, patience, and so much work. Sometimes those dances make us cry.

But they're so important.

It would be easy to deny ourselves the opportunities we have to learn our own dances. To deny that a story shared could be one we can learn from. To deny the opportunity to reflect, and to grow.

"Easy" isn't really what we need, though. In a society structured around convenience, built for those quick dopamine hits, it's an act of courage to choose the harder work of reflection, patience, and—at times—pain.

It's so, incredibly, wildly, worth it.

Adrienne, Socrates, and my mother are and were all of the same mind in this one way: Life is an experiment. You have basic elements, which in Adrienne's book starts with formative years and family origins. Whether Adrienne's own story, which she shares so vulnerably, matches your own in obvious ways, or whether you need to dig a little to find the parallels, the steps she takes to grow into the person I have come to know and deeply value are all steps you can take, with your friend Adrienne at your side.

Through her journey in the pages of this book, Adrienne takes the time to reflect on how each moment, each stage, each learning helps her know herself. She asks you to reflect in that same way, with important questions which can only be answered by you. Through her stories, we come to understand our own. We know our history. We know our values. We know ourselves.

And we learn to dance.

Julia Y. Chung, CFP®, CLU, FEA, TEP
CEO, Financial Planner &
Family Enterprise Advisor

Introduction

Your current position in life results from the millions of choices you have made over a lifetime. This book helps you uncover the reasons behind your choices and discover why you are where you are right now.

I am a woman in my sixties. I have made some tough choices in my life—choices that hurt people I love. I have endured a lot of adversity because of my choices. At times this adversity was so overwhelming, I didn't want to get out of bed to face another day. I refer to these as *Duvet Days*, the days when adversity took me to my knees, and I wondered if I could take another step.

Adversity has also been a blessing. Adversity has been the impetus for putting my life back on track, transporting me to a place where I am happy in love, surrounded by family and friends who love me, and doing what I am passionate about in my career. Many painful ups and downs have helped me discover what makes me dance. I share my experiences and lessons learned. By sharing my journey, my goal is to help you discover the true essence of who you are and what makes you dance, so you can dance your own path to joy and inner peace.

Almost twenty years ago, I had a spiritual experience that was so profound and lasting, it prompted me to write this book. I was struggling with a choice in my career. While walking with my dog, Rox, in a breathtaking rainforest located in British Columbia, Canada, I heard a voice from within ask: *What makes you dance?*

This simple question helped me rediscover who I am. Learning what makes me dance has been a process that began by understanding where I came from. By unravelling my past and sifting and sorting my past experiences, I was able to discover which experiences worked for me and which experiences no longer served me. I realized I was making choices that were based on past experiences and outdated beliefs people had imposed on me. These old beliefs were more about the other people than they were about me.

Through the process of consciously understanding why I made certain choices, I was able to understand what got me where I am. As a young mom, I was sometimes unhappy, feeling stuck, unseen, and lost. Through a lot of soul-searching, pain, and adversity, I discovered why I was making certain choices. Once I understood why, I was able to make different ones. Today, I am happy and fulfilled, and every part of my life makes me dance.

I have raised four strong-willed daughters. This has been my greatest accomplishment and my greatest challenge. Being a mother is the most rewarding and the most thankless job there is. I have questioned who I am as a mother, a wife, friend, daughter, sister, business owner, career woman, and person in this world. I lost myself in motherhood, tackled a lot of self-doubt, and questioned many outdated beliefs to rediscover myself. As a mom, I was the glue for everyone else, and I became stuck. Motherhood changed me.

You Are Here

Most of us as mothers start out with little training and find ourselves making it up as we go along. Have you heard the expression *fake it till you make it*? That's what I did. As a mother, I faked it until I made it every day. Raising kids shaped me in ways that were difficult to imagine amid all the demands and chaos that motherhood entails. This is my story, and if you are reading this book, it's probably part of your story too.

I am divorced and one of the lucky ones who, after divorce, found the *love of my life*. I am now part of a blended family with seven fabulous adult children, wonderful partners and married-ins, and a growing number of grandchildren. The path to get here was both gut-wrenching and joyful. I often told myself if I didn't laugh, I would cry—so I chose to do both.

The Three-Circle Model and You

Buckle up as we journey together into the past to uncover the reasons behind the choices we have made that brought us here.

The concepts in this book are based on a Venn diagram, in this case, a three-circle model.

The Three-Circle Model

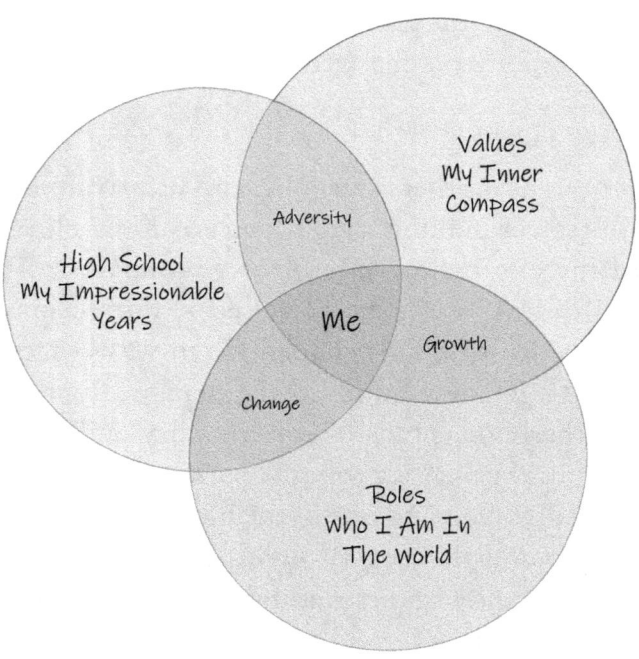

*Connect the Dots: unravel the fabric of your life to
rediscover what makes you dance.*

The three-circle model is fluid and consists of
overlapping circles that are always at play with one
another. At any time, adversity can strike and will
create change and, we hope, growth. Each one of us
is right in the middle of it all, weathering life amid all
these complexities, not knowing what will happen next.

By sharing my story, I hope to inspire you to re-discover your story. I share different methods of self-refection and self-discovery that have helped me unravel parts of myself. Visit my website at www.unravelyou.com, where I share my own journey of self-reflection and self-discovery using the same methods. The journey can be difficult at times; know I have gone before you. You will peel back the layers to discover what makes you dance and how you will share your light in the world.

Your journey is unique to you. Self-discovery is meant to happen in bite-sized pieces. You may find, as many others do, the hours or days between times of self-reflection are when you will have moments of clarity.

Thoughts can swirl around in our minds and seem overwhelming because they take on a life of their own. Thoughts on paper are far more manageable. On paper, it's possible to regain control and tackle one thought at a time. Give yourself permission to be curious—curious about you. Keep a journal to record your thoughts.

The time you take to answer questions and follow the prompts in the Your Turn sections at the end of each chapter is your time. For the best use of these sections, sit comfortably in a place with no distractions. Write your responses without reading them; let the words flow from your mind onto paper without judgment. Wisdom lives within all of us. This is your time to discover and reflect upon the wisdom that lives within you.

The thoughts you put down on paper are for your eyes only; this is not a test. Do your best to write your thoughts freely, without inhibition. Write like no one is watching, and know that no one will read your words unless you want them to.

I provide you with questions designed to build upon one another, and they might reveal patterns and insight that surprise you. Mark with a coloured pen; use circles or underlines to accentuate thoughts that stand out. Make note of any themes. This is a way of unravelling who you are and how you got here, one thread at a time. Self-discovery and self-reflection take strength and courage, and the journey can be enlightening and transformational.

The circles of the Venn diagram represent:

High School – My Impressionable Years: These are the years that provide the foundation for all our lives. The impressionable years include high school, the early lessons our parents taught us, the first kiss, our first love, first working experiences, and new friendships, to mention a few. These complex years are full of new experiences that shape us and impact us. By unravelling this time, we can discover which experiences work for us and which experiences no longer serve us.

Values – My Inner Compass: Our values form in the impressionable years. Our interactions with family, friends, teachers, and co-workers affect how our inner beliefs form. Our first experiences in work, love, and play shape how we see the world. Unaware, we develop our own perspective about life, and this perspective guides our behaviours and becomes our inner compass. Values become deeply rooted within us and act as our internal compass. Our values are active in every aspect of our life.

Roles – Who I Am in the World: Who we are as a mom, sister, friend, career woman, business owner, daughter, aunt, cousin, or partner is the result of our values and experiences that have shaped us in our impressionable years. Who we are in the world is linked to how we feel about ourselves. Certain roles bring us closer to our authentic selves, and other roles can take us further away. When the distance between our authentic self and the person we feel the need to portray is vast, we can feel a sense of uneasiness. We know when who we are in the world feels right and when it doesn't. It's a feeling that comes from deep within. To add to the complexity, at any time, a current experience can trigger an experience from our past and cause us to act in a certain way. With awareness of these past triggers, we can simply acknowledge their existence without being controlled by them.

Adversity: Adversity can strike and knock us to the ground. When adversity strikes, we draw on our past experiences and our values to move through the dark forest of adversity toward the light that exists on the other side. Adversity has the power to keep us stuck, and it has the power to transform and change us.

Change: Change happens along the journey through the dark forest to the light on the other side. Most people see the world differently than they did before adversity struck. Adversity carries a silver lining of transformational change that is difficult to discover until we reach the light and have time to recover and reflect.

Growth: The silver lining is growth. Adversity brings newfound awareness and appreciation when we let it. Each one of us possesses the ability to stay stuck in adversity or to learn and grow from it. My faith grew in adversity, and that was the greatest gift of all.

Me: You are here, right in the middle of these intersecting, constantly moving and interplaying circles. Sometimes, it's difficult to be human, contending with all these hidden forces that influence our behaviours. Unravelling your three circles and reflecting upon the impact of the interplay of these dynamics are the keys to figuring out what makes you dance.

When you trust the process, life takes you to places you previously could only have imagined. Every choice you make in your life contributes to the fabric of your life. Your choices may take you down roads you don't anticipate. Sometimes you find yourself in a good place, and sometimes your choices lead you to places where you feel lost and alone. When you unravel the fabric of your life and understand the origin of your choices, you can discover which choices work for you and which no longer serve you.

Maybe you're reading this book because it's time to let go of old choices and embrace new ones. It's possible to rewrite your story. Your choices have brought you to this place. Your past choices don't have to define you forever.

I invite you to join a community of like-minded individuals from all over the world who want to grow and make a difference. See the Sharing Your Light section at the back of the book to sign up for our email list and receive stories of hope, hints for surviving and thriving in motherhood, and connections with people like you. At www.unravelyou.com/game, you can also learn about the board game I created called *Now You're Talking* to inspire people to discuss and share experiences from their impressionable years, their values, their roles in the world, and their times of adversity and change. Sometimes life's difficulties are a little easier to bear when we help one another by sharing stories of hope and celebration.

Congratulate yourself for having the courage to start the process. Put away your to-do list for now. This is your time to disconnect from the world and your devices and reconnect with yourself.

Let's get started.

Chapter One

High School ~
The Impressionable Years

You may be thinking high school is an odd place to start the journey of self-discovery. High school is something most of us have in common, even though our high school experiences are as individual as we are.

I am an executive recruiter; *headhunting* is a term that's also used to describe what I do. I contribute to building leadership teams within entrepreneurial companies. It's like *The Dating Game* in business. Owners of companies share who they are looking for; I go to the market and find the match.

I have been working with a process called *Topgrading* for over fifteen years. Topgrading starts by asking candidates questions about their high school years. The founders of Topgrading believe high school experiences repeat throughout a person's career. After conducting hundreds of interviews with candidates, I have grown to understand that not only do our experiences during that impressionable time impact our careers, they also influence every aspect of our life, forever.

I understand not everyone has attended high school. For those of you who haven't attended high school, when I refer to that time, think of your impressionable years when you experienced a lot of firsts. It is a time that contributes greatly to the fabric of your life. It's a time when many of us learn life lessons that play out again and again. When I hear people's answers to my questions about low points or times of adversity in the impressionable years, this provides me insight into how a candidate will respond to adversity today.

Think about your experiences from that time. If you're like most people, your mind instantly travelled back in time. In my high school days, interactions in the cafeteria represented a social pecking order, and no one challenged the absurdity of it all. We all conformed. The *cool kids* sat at the front of the cafeteria, and the level of perceived coolness descended from there, right to the back of the cafeteria where the not-so-cool kids sat huddled in the back row. Our position within this social structure contributes to how we see ourselves in the world throughout our lives. Although this time contributes to shaping our perspective about who we are and how we show up in life, it doesn't define us.

On my first day of high school, my older brother, Jim, was starting grade thirteen and coached me on what to wear. Jim told me to wear something that looked like it had been worn for a long time. He told me I didn't want to look like I tried too hard. I wore an old, red-and-white striped T-shirt, ripped jeans, and well-worn running shoes. My goal was to look like I was too cool to care about what I was wearing. My appearance was a lie. I left my bedroom looking like a tornado hit, with layers and layers of discarded clothing choices strewn all over my bed and bedroom floor.

The high school journey began. Unwritten rule number one: Manage my image and never let *them* see me sweat. In high school, I discovered the power of the first impression. I was aware of my appearance and what my appearance said about me. I also perfected the swan façade: calm and cool above the water, but below, paddling madly to survive.

This first-day experience is different for everyone. I was fortunate an older brother could pave my way. My starting high school was a new dynamic my brother felt necessary to manage. Until his sister arrived on the scene, Jim had had the run of the place and had only his image to worry about. Because I was new on Jim's high school turf, I could potentially damage his reputation, so Jim influenced my first impression the best he could. Not only did Jim tell me how to dress on my first day, he also told me how to greet people in the hall.

I continue to consider what I wear and the message my clothing conveys about me. I chose a profession in which a person's first impression has an impact on their future. Candidates have a better chance of moving forward in the hiring process when their first impression is positive.

High school is a place full of complexities and unknown experiences, and most of us muddle through, just hoping to survive. High school is a breeding ground of new learning experiences that contribute to the foundation of who we are. For this reason, we delve a little deeper to better understand the root cause of some of the choices we have made or continue to make in our life.

High School Stories That Shape Us

When I was in high school, I told a very private and confidential story about my best friend, Nova, to the biggest gossip in high school. In no time, this story was all over the school in a new, more sensationalized way. I betrayed Nova's trust and almost lost a cherished friendship that remains central to my life today. This experience shaped me and continues to impact how I behave in the world. Today, I won't share what someone has told me in confidence because I know the consequences are devastating.

We are all mosaics, made up of many pieces. Some pieces take up more space and certain pieces no longer fit. Some pieces play havoc and hold us back. High school is a significant piece for most. My goal is to help you discover and accept the significant pieces of your mosaic and how the pieces impact where and who you are in the world. Here are a few stories for illustration.

Story One: Daphne

Daphne was a courageous young woman whose spouse had accepted a position in Canada. It was time for her to establish the next step in her career. In our interview, I asked Daphne about a low point during high school. She told me she came from a family of lawyers and politicians. Throughout her childhood, her parents had encouraged her to follow a similar path. They assumed Daphne's career would fall in step, and she, too, would choose politics or law as a profession. Daphne had known from a very young age these professions did not fuel her passion. She loved science.

As difficult as it was, Daphne stood her ground and went against family tradition. To stay true to herself, Daphne required post-secondary education in science at a very expensive university. Her parents refused to support her. With steadfast determination, she found a way; she asked her grandmother for financial support and eventually won the support of her entire family.

For Daphne, this pattern of staying true to herself—and in the process, helping those around her see the world differently—became central to who she is. In her career, Daphne makes decisions that are best for a company. These decisions cause people to change their behaviour and see the world differently. Because most people don't like change, Daphne is often met with resistance, much like the resistance she felt from her family in high school. Daphne's early experience provided the foundation for her professional success. She proved she was capable of changing people's perspectives. In her career, she inspires and guides people though the process of change so they may embrace new and more effective ways.

Had Daphne's experience been different in the impressionable years, her life could have gone in a different direction. She possessed the courage to chart her own path and found a career that aligned with that experience. When Daphne made the decision to immigrate to Canada—leaving friends and family behind—once again, she unintentionally encouraged people to see the world from her curious perspective. Daphne had the courage in high school to stay true to what she felt was right, even when people around her were resistant to change. Daphne has continued to demonstrate this resilience throughout her life.

Story Two: Olivia

Olivia lived in Germany, where students at the young age of fourteen are pigeonholed into one of three categories: The first category is for those deemed worthy of going to university. University is perceived as being more academic and more theoretical and is for students who find studying and learning easy. Students in the second category go to college. College teaches skills that are more practical, and it is perceived to be a place for students who may struggle academically. The third category is reserved for those destined for trades, such as plumbing, electrical, or hairstyling, to name a few. Studying the trades is the most practical and hands-on education of all. Social status within the high school system is closely linked to academic achievement. The *cool kids* go to university, and the rest of the kids are looked down upon.

Much to Olivia's surprise and horror, she was told she fit into category number two and was destined for college. People she had thought were her friends shunned her and continue to do so. Whether because of societal norms, cruel high school rules about status, or a combination of the two, she felt she could no longer stay at that school. Returning to the country roots of one of her parents and where she was born, Olivia packed her bag, and at age sixteen with only one hundred dollars in her pocket, she arrived in Canada without speaking a word of English.

Olivia's motivation was to *show them*. She set out to prove she was as good as the people she had left behind. Her resilience has been an essential survival skill throughout her life. Olivia has created a life in Canada that started from nothing. It has taken courage, strength, and enormous resilience to build a successful life—one that many would envy. Olivia's resilience appeared as the result of a tumultuous high school experience, and it was that experience that triggered a series of events that has changed the course of her life.

Story Three: David

David was bullied in high school. He told his father about the incident, and his father told him to go back to school and stand up for himself. His father believed being bullied was a sign of weakness, and he wasn't tolerating *weakness* in his son. David did what his father asked: stood up for himself—and was badly beaten. Through this experience, David developed both toughness and emotional intelligence.

In his current work life, David must defend decisions regularly and back his decisions with confidence. He must also keep people moving forward and challenge the status quo. David is asked to *stand up to* colleagues who would much rather resist change. Part of his survival in the impressionable years was to understand the reasons behind the bully's behaviour. What his father had perceived as a weakness became David's strength. Standing up and using brute force did not make David an effective leader; instead, his ability to understand the motivation behind behaviour inspires people to change.

Life Lessons From High School

High school memories—high points, low points, and influences in those impressionable years—shape us; they don't have to define us. People remember high school in an instant, regardless of age. Even if we want to forget our high school experiences, these memories stay with us.

Many candidates I work with are not born in Canada, and school systems vary depending on where people are from. Despite different educational systems, I have discovered the emotion people carry from high school is similar.

Behaviours that begin in the impressionable years can easily become entrenched within us. My daughter's kindergarten teacher once said she enjoyed seeing the essence of who a child is in kindergarten. Even by the end of elementary school, however, this essence starts to hide behind protective walls. These walls are a part of the survival skills we develop to reserve our sense of self. Maybe someone laughs at us or calls us a name, tells us we are not good at math, or we can't draw or sing. We cast doubt upon ourselves at a very young age. Understanding the impact of those impressionable years triggers unravelling the fabric of our life to rediscover our true essence.

When I was in high school, the classic cliques existed. We had the jocks, the nerds, the band kids, the cool kids, and a group we called the "rampers," the kids who would smoke between classes out by the ramp.

High school was a positive experience. I was fortunate to be part of a large group of friends, mostly jocks. Nova was a cheerleader and seemed to me to be the most athletic of us all. I played basketball throughout high school. I was far from the best athlete, but I was surrounded by very talented athletes, and we won City Championships and the Western Provincials. While athletics didn't define me, I was drawn to sports because of the social connection. Social connections continue to drive me today.

I do have one regret from that time. A group of my friends and I were mean to a girl we believed didn't belong. I was the messenger. I regret not standing up to the group and doing the right thing by celebrating our differences. Back then, surviving the social scene depended upon conforming. Knowing what I know now, I would go back and change my behaviour. I would summon up the courage to tell my friends what we were doing was wrong. Decades later, I phoned this girl and apologized, and even then, she told me about the pain she felt and how that experience changed her life. She wouldn't accept my apology.

I regret I inflicted pain, and this high school experience has inspired me to become more compassionate. I began to trust my intuition in high school and learned I could resist going along with the group. It takes courage to stand up, and it took my lack of courage to realize how important doing the right thing is, especially when a person's well-being is at stake. Seeds of wisdom germinate in the high school years and can provide valuable clues for discovering who we are.

Receiving a secret from a trusted friend is a privilege and a sacred bond. Breaking this bond could have had devastating results for me. High school can be a microcosm full of impulsive, hormone-driven teenagers whose brains are still forming. It is amazing any of us have survived it, let alone having learned some of the richest and most life-altering lessons. *Go Lions!*

Your Turn: The Impressionable Years

In your journal, list three stories that stand out for you in high school. Recall these stories in detail. Why do these stories stand out? How does each story influence your behaviour today?

	Description	This story stands out because:	This story affects my behaviour today:
Story 1			
Story 2			
Story 3			

Insights:
Highlight three words or phrases from your time in high school that contribute in a positive way to the fabric of your life:

1.
2.
3.

Reframe:

Rewrite the three points above in a way that speaks to you today:

1.
2.
3.

Unravel More:

Use this table to further explore your stories.

	If I could go back to high school, what would I do differently?	If I could go back to high school, what would I do the same?	What advice would I give recent high school graduates?
Story 1			
Story 2			
Story 3			

More Insights:

Highlight three words or phrases from your answers that represent lessons you take forward and contribute in a positive way to who you are in the world.

Reframe:

Write a sentence combining these three words or phrases that speaks to you today: _____.

Please complete this sentence:

The number one lesson I learned in high school that still applies today is:_____.

Chapter Two

Outside the School Walls

People come into our lives for a reason, a season, or a lifetime. When I look back, I recognize there were significant people who changed the course of my life. For me, one was Nova. We met in grade five and became friends immediately. Growing up in the seventies was different than it is now. The world seemed safer. Our parents were the opposite of helicopter parents. Nova and I would leave our houses in the morning, and as long as we returned before dark, our parents didn't worry. There were no cell phones and no way to stay in contact. Nova and I developed our own buddy system and watched out for each other.

Because Nova and I grew up together, we experienced a lot of firsts together and have formed many of the same habits that originated back then. Even though Canada separates us, when we get together, we discover we still share beliefs, actions, and attitudes—a direct result of spending so much time together growing up.

People who come into our lives in our growing years shape us and influence our decisions and behaviours throughout life. By reflecting on both the positive and negative influences, we can better understand how past experiences influence our decisions today. Friends, teachers, siblings, and strangers we met during the impressionable years influence us even now.

The world around us is fluid. The right person seems to appear in our lives when the time is right.

How Parents Shape Us

Parents make decisions that come from their beliefs. Their behaviours, choices, and words impact us as we grow, and they continue to influence us into our adulthood. My dad believed women should be "barefoot, pregnant, and in the kitchen." Even as I write this, I cringe. The kitchen was the last place I wanted to be.

Having four daughters born so close together, I probably did spend a lot of my younger years barefoot, pregnant, and in the kitchen. This is a choice I made. It took me decades to break free from the female stereotype my dad taught me. It was difficult in my teenage years to differentiate between my own truth and my dad's truth. I trusted him and believed what he said.

My dad's beliefs were based on his story, and they were more about him than they were about me, yet I took on my dad's truth as my own. It took years of journaling, therapy, and self-reflection to finally accept that my dad's truth was his, not mine. This new awareness helped me counteract the beliefs my dad had about women in general. My dad's beliefs influenced many of my life decisions in my twenties and thirties.

Family dynamics and high school dynamics together shape us as individuals. It's the converging of the two that make this time in our lives so influential. We are given our families to learn the lessons we need to learn. This prepares us and teaches us lessons we need to fulfill our purpose.

My family shaped me and my friends saved me.

My dad was a dominant member of our family; he made the rules. My mom let my dad make most of the decisions. It was a sign of the times. I am the only daughter between two strong-willed brothers, Jim and Max. Being the only daughter in a household where men were encouraged to dominate was challenging. It was sometimes difficult to be heard, and I often felt unsafe voicing my opinion because I feared being ridiculed. I mastered the art of deflection, a survival skill I perfected for my self-preservation.

I was born two months premature and was perceived as weak because I was often sick in my early childhood. I'm not sure if I was perceived as being weak because I was a girl, or because I came out of the womb faster than most. Arriving in this world in 1959, weighing less than four pounds and surviving when medicine wasn't as advanced showed strength, determination, and a lack of patience. From my perspective, it is a miracle I survived, and I had something to prove.

As I was growing up, my parents reinforced strict boundaries regarding male and female roles. My dad worked and was the provider, and my mom stayed at home to raise us. From a very young age, I set out to challenge these roles, and my parents responded exactly how I expected. My mom would insist I make my bed, yet she would make my brothers' beds. This seemed unfair. My brothers were happy; their rooms were always in perfect order—my mom made sure of it. I decided to push the boundaries and continually leave my room in a disastrous state to see what would happen. I would close my door, and eventually my mom would clean my room too. I was defying my mom's perspective and how she saw the world. In a small way, I was challenging the inequities between men and women. In hindsight, had we all been given the responsibility to clean our own rooms, I wouldn't have felt the need to push back on the imbalance of rules that was based on gender and outdated stereotypes.

High School Experiences Become Part of You

Every day, I make it my mission to combat the inequities between men and women. As an executive recruiter, I ask people what they expect for compensation. Men state a number with no excuses. Women often have difficulty answering the question. Once I pull out a number, women apologetically tell me "It's not about the money," it's about the team, the culture, and the fit. Generally, women have difficulty valuing what they bring to the table. I find myself coaching women to understand how men see the world differently. Women bring so much value to the workplace, and even today, women continually sell themselves short. When we women embrace our value and stop being our own worst enemies, the world will become a better place.

When I'm coaching women, I am reminded of the feelings I had as a kid, when my mom gave my brothers special treatment because "they are boys." Our families and the dynamics we endure growing up inspire how we make a difference in the world.

One day when I was around fourteen, my dad and my brother were deciding what to have for lunch. My dad asked me to make them each a sandwich. I responded by saying "make your own sandwiches." My dad, in an attempt to put me back into the traditional female role, said "your mother wouldn't say that." These two seemingly insignificant situations are experiences that took me away from my true essence. I felt there was something wrong with me because I didn't fit the traditional female mold my parents had embraced.

I internalized this expectation and tried desperately to be the *woman* my parents wanted me to be. I married and had children with Stu, someone who, much like my father, was very happy when I was in a subservient role supporting him. Stu could leave on business trips knowing everything was looked after on the home front. Night after night we spoke of his career and his aspirations. Even though I enjoyed this conversation because it gave me the opportunity to focus on business, I was living vicariously through Stu's experiences and was kept on the sidelines. As Stu's career soared and he became more of who he wanted to be, I became increasingly less of myself. I didn't have an identity. I was my daughter's mother, my husband's wife, or even my dog's owner. My name was gone and I became invisible.

Your Great Influences in Your Impressionable Years

Journaling and self-reflection can be difficult. It can also be freeing because it shines a light on secrets you may have hidden from yourself. In the darkness, these secrets take on a life of their own and impact decisions we make. Secrets, when exposed on paper, lose power.

When you read something you wrote that surprises you, approach it with curiosity. Instead of feeling bad about yourself, simply look at the words on paper and say: *that's interesting*. The word *interesting* is just that. What you write isn't bad or good; it just is.

Journaling is meant to give you insight into the choices you made in your life. Every time you discover something that causes you to pause and reflect, you have unravelled another thread of your life. Every thread is a pathway to wisdom and inner peace. Begin the process of letting go of thoughts and experiences that no longer serve you. Keep the thoughts that take you closer to what makes you dance. Unravelling who you are and how you got here can be painful. Trust the process and know it's worth it in the end.

Keep going.

Your Turn: My Great Influences

Think about the person who influenced you the most in your impressionable years. As you journal and reflect, be kind to yourself. Make a table in your journal that looks like this, and jot down who comes to mind:

	Who was my greatest influence in the impressionable years?	What did this person teach me?	How did this person influence my decisions and who I am today?	How does this person contribute to what makes me uniquely me?	What would I like to say to this person?
Person 1					
Person 2					
Person 3					

Insight:

Now circle the answers above that stand out. List three insights you've gained below.

These people have taught me:

1.
2.
3.

They've contributed to my development by:
    1.
    2.
    3.

Reframe:
Look at the insights you've gained and the influences that have made you uniquely you and complete the sentence below in your journal:

It is my _____ that makes me uniquely me.

Chapter Three

Adversity Strikes and Shines Its Light

Adversity hit our family with a crushing blow. One morning at seven o'clock, I received a call from my mom and my life changed in an instant. My dad had died suddenly at age fifty-eight. My parents had just closed their house and were en route to Florida, where they were going to spend time contemplating their retirement chapter. Ironically, my dad was incorporating an in-depth health checkup on their trip. Just an hour from my parent's house, their car stopped working. My mom placed a HELP sign on the window. Some kind stranger quickly came to my parents' rescue and took them to a service station. There, my dad suffered a dissecting aortic aneurism. He died shortly after he arrived at the hospital.

Our lives changed forever. My dad had a big influence on the choices we made, and without him, we were forced to make our own choices. More than thirty years later, I realize life would have turned out differently had my dad lived: It took my dad's death for me to question my life and the choices I had made. I became closer to God because I had to believe I would see my dad again.

My dad's death prompted a journey that took me back to the essence of who I am, not the person my parents wanted me to be. In a weird way, when my dad died, I no longer felt the need to make the choices he wanted me to make. I made choices that were right for me. My dad's death was the beginning of a journey that brought me back to me.

This process didn't happen overnight; it took years.

Life's tragedies have a way of getting us back on course. Adversity was my wakeup call. For thirty-one years, my life had gone according to plan. Whether it began as my plan or a plan my parents had ingrained in me, I made it my own, and it became a part of me. When my dad died, my life turned upside down. Life didn't prepare me for someone I love to be here one day and, without warning, to be gone the next.

My dad's death sparked something inside me. In the instant I received that phone call, the world was different; my naivety was gone. For a long time after, I would observe people having fun and wonder how they could be happy when I felt such despair. My eyes still well up with tears. The time immediately following his death taught me to be more empathetic and to show compassion toward others who are experiencing loss.

Until I experienced loss of this magnitude, I had no idea how all-consuming the feelings of loss and grief are.

The Power of Grief

I gained insight into how people grieve differently. My mom and my brothers all grieved differently. Grief on this scale was new to us, and we had to find our own way of coping with our new reality. We each had to create our *new normal* individually.

I coped with my grief by sharing my feelings with Nova and my sister-in-law, E, who was married to my brother Jim. E was the sister I never had. E shared an uncommon understanding of our family dynamics from the inside and an accepting, nonjudgmental perspective. We would talk for hours; it was therapeutic.

I remember saying good-bye to my dad for the last time. My dad lay motionless, expressionless, in the coffin. The person I knew was gone. Someone I love lying inside an open casket is something I am unable to un-see.

I thought I was alone in the room experiencing something I didn't think I would have to face for decades. Jim, Max, and my mom were outside the room. The process of dealing with our grief in separate ways had begun. I turned to leave the room, devastated and feeling alone, and there was E, standing about ten feet behind me, silently holding my coat. E knew when I needed space and knew when I needed support. In that moment, E gave me both.

And then, adversity struck our family again. E was scheduled to visit me in two days on the West Coast, and I was excited to see her. The rhododendrons were in full bloom, and I knew E would love to experience the coast in May. Suddenly and without warning, I received the phone call saying E was rushed to the hospital because of her heart. E had a heart condition that took her life a few days later, at age twenty-seven. Although I only knew E for four years, she has been with me every day since. I'm thankful E was in my life, even for a short time. The loss of my dad and E in the same year changed the way I viewed the world. It felt at that point like my life was divided into two sections: the life I had with my dad and E in it and the new life I needed to recreate without them.

Adversity powerfully and painfully moved my life in a different direction—a direction I didn't imagine for myself. The death of my dad and E caused me to look deep within and ask myself who I was and whether I was happy.

With my dad and E gone, I had no one within my family to turn to. I didn't want to burden my brothers or my mom with my grief. We were maneuvering through our own pain. For the first time, it was clear I had married someone who was incapable of support and emotional connection. Adversity brought the emotional void in my marriage clearly into light. Before my new reality, I naturally connected with my dad and E when I needed to speak with someone in my family about what was happening in my life—until I couldn't.

A few months after my dad and E were gone, my mom came out west to visit. I felt like I was coping well with the loss. My mom thought differently. I was going through the motions and had lost my sparkle. When my mom returned home, I received a call from my brother Jim. Jim and my mom had spoken, and after their conversation, Jim decided to send me money from E's account for grief counselling. Jim said E would have wanted me to have it.

After my dad died, I tried to go to grief counselling in a group setting. My grief was so close to the surface, I found myself sobbing uncontrollably in front of a group of strangers. That experience scared me from trying grief counselling again. With my mom and Jim's encouragement, I gave one-on-one grief counselling a try. Although it was easier, I didn't benefit a lot from the counselling. Because I wasn't experiencing suicidal thoughts, I felt my grief wasn't a top priority for the counsellor.

The value I gained from counselling came from my ability to muster the courage to go to counselling. For the first time, I was making my grief a priority instead of telling myself I was okay. I began to accept my grief was real and all consuming.

Grief counselling helped me realize I was dealing with three deaths, the third being the pending doom of my marriage. In my time of grief, I experienced Stu's inability to support me the way I needed. I felt alone in my grief. At my lowest point, Stu shared he no longer wanted to kiss me.

Six years into our marriage, with me in the depths of mourning, Stu informed me kissing was something he no longer liked, and kissing between us was a thing of the past. That unexpected and unimaginable news struck a blow. Adversity and grief had exposed our relationship for what it really was: an emotionless façade, void of passion.

I realized I hadn't dealt with my dad's death, and when E passed suddenly, I dealt with an accumulation of sadness that weighed me down. I went through the motions to get through another day. The void of losing someone doesn't go away, it dissipates over time. Grief lives below the surface and can be triggered at any time.

Writing this book has brought back memories I thought I had managed to set free a long time ago, only to have tears streaming down my face decades later. Grief is the price we pay for being vulnerable and loving with our whole heart. Loving this big takes courage. Surviving the pain I felt when my dad and E were gone took gut-wrenching strength and determination to put one foot in front of the other.

Feeling Connected in Grief

Determined to be a good mom, I powered on, even though I felt sick inside. I filled my days with fun adventures with my girls. My life was in constant chaos. The delivery of my third daughter was a difficult birth that ended well but had come perilously close to disaster. I was sent home from the hospital while my baby had to stay in neonatal care.

The thought of leaving her behind at the hospital made me feel sick—like I would be leaving a part of myself behind. Stu was too busy at work to pick me up. My mom was busy at home with my two older daughters, Reese and Kendra. I had no choice but to call a taxi.

Something told me to reach into the overnight bag I had brought with me to the hospital. It was a bag that had belonged to E. Much to my amazement, I found an old gym card with E's picture on it. In that moment, I knew E was with me and I was no longer alone. I decided to name my newest daughter after E: Eve.

Adversity shapes us and changes us. Moments like these contribute to the fabric of our lives. That moment and many moments since, I have felt my dad and E are watching over me. It's like they are in the next room with a one-way mirror. They can see me, but I can't see them.

Getting to the other side of adversity and grief is a difficult journey that is rich with insight and lessons. I was different on the other side of adversity. Grief left its mark that transformed me. Experiencing this enormous loss was the beginning of change, change that brought me closer to my true essence and opened me to having a relationship with God.

When my dad and E were no longer here to support me, the truth of my relationship with Stu was revealed. Adversity shone a light and let me in on some secrets I had been hiding from myself. Adversity and grief connected me to what was really going on and brought me closer to my inner self and what I longed for in my marriage.

Adversity is an overwhelming, all-consuming, and unforgiving beast. It is powerful and unrelenting and can take us out of life for a while. It's difficult to imagine the pain will eventually subside and we will feel normal again. If you are dealing with adversity and grief, my heart goes out to you. Adversity sucks when we're in it. Be kind to yourself; your whole being is evolving, and this takes courage and energy to endure.

Although getting my thoughts down on paper helped the process of transformation, sometimes journaling was too painful. I found it helpful to go for a walk in nature instead. Taking time to notice flowers, the blue sky, the all-knowing trees, helped me to believe my pain was part of a bigger purpose. I did my best to breathe deeply, but sometimes that was too hard. Putting one foot in front of the other is the goal. Keep moving forward in some way.

If journaling is too difficult, simply think about these questions instead. Put your thoughts on paper when you're ready. This is not a race; it's an individual journey of growth and change. Be compassionate with yourself, and as you move forward, one step at a time, trust the process. You will get to the other side, transformed, and the pain will dissipate with time.

Your Turn: Understanding the Impact of Adversity

Use the table below to further explore the impact of adversity.

	Adversity came into my life when:	Adversity transformed me in this way:	Adversity led me to these insights:	Adversity revealed this about me:	Adversity revealed this about my situation:
Situation 1					
Situation 2					
Situation 3					

Insights:

Highlight, circle, or underline thoughts from the chart above that stand out. List those thoughts below.

1.
2.
3.

Reframe:

How did adversity transform me?

Put these thoughts into a sentence or two that speaks to you today: _____

Chapter Four

Values ~ The Inner Compass

I was always determined to have four children. For me the leap from one to two children was huge. Two to three and three to four made my life busier and more chaotic. Chaos was something I grew to love.

When I was pregnant with Mila, my fourth daughter, I was over the age of thirty-five and was encouraged to have an amniocentesis, an invasive procedure requiring a needle to be inserted into the abdomen to extract a sample of the amniotic fluid. This test determines the probability the baby will have Down's syndrome. I felt this test was too invasive and opted for a less intrusive, less accurate test.

The results surprised me. I had a 25 percent—a one-in-four—chance of having a child with Down's. Throughout our marriage I had said I would have an abortion if there was any chance a child would struggle with health issues. As it happened, the day I received the results of the test was the same day I had been to the doctor for an ultrasound. I had seen the four cavities of Mila's heart on the screen. Once I witnessed the miracle of life growing within me, an abortion was out of the question.

To compromise, I reluctantly had an amniocentesis. Everything was fine—once again, everything, except my marriage. For three weeks, we co-existed in icy silence. Stu felt I had betrayed him. I was already picturing myself raising my four daughters on my own. Intuitively, I knew our marriage was over.

That experience taught me a very important lesson. Before I was faced with the reality of abortion, my perspective had been naive. I flippantly imagined I could make the decision easily. Until I was faced with reality, I didn't understand the magnitude of this life-or-death decision and how significantly it would affect me. I questioned past decisions, my current situation, and my beliefs. In those three weeks, I became more compassionate toward myself and more compassionate toward other women who are faced with this decision. I discovered strength I didn't know I had. The She-Lion showed herself from deep within me, and I knew I would protect Mila no matter what.

In retrospect, I see Stu's values and my values were misaligned. I have grown to understand that when values between two people are out of alignment, eventually the relationship crumbles. This applies to spouses, business partners, friendships, work colleagues, and, sometimes, even families. Relationships grow stronger when values are aligned. The opposite is true; when values are out of alignment, eventually people drift apart.

Time and reflection have provided flashes of wisdom that I could not have seen in the moment. When my emotions were high and chaos was the norm, my approach was more about survival than clarity. Now, decades later, I can reflect and see the moments when the cracks appeared in my marriage. These cracks eventually turned into divides too vast to fix. There were pattens in our relationship that had formed long before we were married. I didn't see these patterns because I was relentless in my goal to have four children. My drive to have four children gave me focus. I had blinders on and refused to see anything that got in the way of my goal. Having four children was my escape; the demands were too great to think of much else.

Six weeks after Mila was born, healthy and energetic, I was at the gym, starting the difficult journey back to a pre-baby state. Six weeks may seem early to start an exercise routine requiring me to leave my daughter in daycare at the gym. My level of anxiety over germs Mila would pick up from other infants was minimal in comparison to the fear I felt about germs with my first daughter, Reese. With three older sisters in elementary school and pre-school, Mila was exposed to a petri dish of germs daily under our own roof.

* * *

One day, it happened. For the first time in eighteen years, I noticed another man. One glance as the elevator opened is all it took, and my life changed forever. It was love at first sight. I could feel a physical shift in my body—like a part of me that had been shut down and closed off sprang to life. To notice another man felt physically different. My reaction surprised and shocked me. It was like something unlocked within me.

I'm not sure what was more surprising: the fact that I hadn't noticed another man in eighteen years, or the impact it had on me physically when I did. I had been so focused on having four children that once I achieved this goal, I was free to see outside the blinders I hadn't known were there. Every feeling I had repressed shone through in that moment. Once I had four children, it was like the flood gates to my feelings were opened, and I could see the world around me and breathe again.

The Paradox of Life

Ethan, the guy I saw in the elevator that day, was both an angel and the impetus that galvanized adversity. The paradox of life: This pivotal moment was both a blessing and a curse. I couldn't begin to imagine the events that would unfold.

Often the universe has different plans for us than we have for ourselves. Adversity shone a light on new pathways and gave me a glimpse of what was possible. Through adversity, I was able to see beyond what I'd imagined. Adversity changed the course of my life and got me back on track. Adversity gave me a glimpse of the life I was meant to live, not the life I believed I was *supposed to* live.

Supposed-Tos and Should-Dos

A *supposed-to* or *should-do* life is based on the expectations of others. A life based on supposed-tos and should-dos is more about the person who is saying these things than it is about the person receiving them.

A life based on how we believe we are meant to live comes from the heart. Living the life I am meant to live has brought me great joy, a feeling of peace in my heart, and a sense of fulfillment.

It was a painful pathway that led me where I am today. At times I needed more courage than I thought I possessed, and I questioned my choices again and again. The pain and the self-doubt were worth it in the end.

I had an affair with Ethan, the *Elevator Guy*. He was five years younger, single, with no children. I was married, in my late thirties with four little daughters under the age of seven. I fell hopelessly in love, and so did he. Our relationship took on a life of its own and changed me profoundly; I am forever thankful. Ethan turned my life and my perspective of who I am upside-down and inside-out.

A once-loyal wife, I was in a steamy relationship with a young unmarried man. Even as I write this, I wonder how it happened. I shudder to think what my life would look like today had I stayed in a passionless relationship with Stu. I would have had one affair after another, searching for the passion and love that was missing. My affair created a crisis. It gave me the wake-up call to accept who I was. My affair shone a light on what I had become unwilling to accept in a relationship. Had I stayed in my marriage with Stu, my soul would have died.

Life was busy and full of necessary distractions that took up my time and focus. Business took Stu away, both physically and emotionally. Stu didn't worry about us when he was away; his entire focus was moving up the corporate ladder and getting ahead in his career. I was the glue that kept it all together on the home front.

I managed what was required to move four times back and forth across the country. While every move coincided with a step up in Stu's career. I lived in a world where kids, pets, packing, unpacking, rebuilding our lives, and looking after my family's well-being demanded my attention. With every move, we had an additional child and the same adaptable, jet-setting dog and cat.

Finding myself in love with another man was unthinkable, and I share later in the book how it took years to forgive myself for my choices.

One evening, I remember leaving to see Ethan. The kids were happy; their babysitter had just arrived. I zoomed out of the garage with my van and crashed into the babysitter's car. I can still hear that sound of crunching metal when I took out the entire right side of her car. I was stunned and in a daze. Understandably, the parents of the babysitter were furious. I continued with my plan to go out; the damage was done.

A week later, I was with my mom, filing an accident report. My mom was driving in front of me. We were at the corner, turning right. I thought my mom had turned right, she hadn't. I plowed right into my mom's car. My mom and I were both fine; our cars were not. The rental car was a write-off, and my mom's car sustained extensive damage.

To further confirm I was under crippling emotional stress, my hair started to fall out in clumps. Although I wouldn't encourage anyone to go through this, having survived it, I feel it all happened for a reason. A counsellor gave me life-affirming advice. She said, "You have a choice. You can stay in your relationship with your husband and deal with the consequences of that, or you can leave your relationship and deal with those consequences. Either way" she said, "there will be consequences."

In that moment, I chose life. I decided I would be an example to my girls as someone who chose to live life with passion, willing to face life with courage and determination. I faced the future without knowing where my life would end up. I was vulnerable and afraid. I was also authentically living my truth for the first time in my life, and it was my truth and my faith that kept me moving forward.

The Teacher Appears When the Student Is Ready

I remember exactly where I was when my girlfriend Allison called and gave me sage advice with encouragement. Allison said, "Ade, jump and the net will appear." This was years after Ethan had come into my life and changed me.

As fate would have it, Stu's career took us west. I left a piece of my heart with Ethan in the East and did my best to keep moving forward with my life. My vision of who I was—who I thought I was supposed to be—no longer existed. My affair with Ethan had shattered everything. Even being the happy mom I once was disappeared for a while. I was consumed with deep, unforgiving despair. I would go to sleep at night praying for God to "pluck me out" of my existence; I didn't know how much more pain I could endure.

I know now that my despair was a part of a letting-go process. Through my deep, unrelenting despair, I journaled every chance I could. Journaling was my attempt to make sense of the swirling thoughts in my head. I gained clarity when I put my thoughts on paper. On paper, my thoughts were less scary, and I was able to put things in perspective. God was probably tired of hearing from me. I prayed and I prayed. In adversity, my faith grew stronger.

Even in my grief, I knew Ethan had come into my life for a reason and a season, not a lifetime. Over time, I became more connected with myself—both who I was and who I was meant to be. Growth started with self-awareness and continued. Adversity was the catalyst for growth. I had lived so many years in denial of my true feelings, once I had a glimpse of what could be, there was no putting the genie back in the bottle.

I received that life-changing call from Allison when I was driving. I was at the top of a steep hill when I answered the phone. When Allison said, "jump and the net will appear," I responded, "I'm jumping."

I decided to make the most difficult decision of my life—to leave my marriage. My decision triggered a series of events. Being at the top of the hill was symbolic, my life went downhill for a long time before it levelled out and started going uphill again.

Messages are all around us. Sometimes we see or hear them, and sometimes we are oblivious to their existence. Maybe this is because we aren't ready to accept the change that follows when we act on these messages. Change is a process of acceptance—acceptance of the current reality and acceptance that something *needs* to change. This takes time. The tipping point happens when the pain of maintaining status quo far outweighs the fear of what the future could hold. In this process of acceptance, *teachers* come into our lives with messages and show us what life can look like when we have the courage to change.

Author Joseph Campbell writes about the Hero's Journey. The archetypal journey includes adversity. In stories that follow this model, the main character is called to transform in some way that is disruptive and daunting. Because change is formidable, the main character often resists change, thinking they can stay safe and secure by maintaining status quo.

Ultimately, the pain of everything remaining the same becomes greater than the fear of the unknown. Then it happens: The main character sees the message that has been there the whole time. Perhaps a mentor or teacher comes into this person's life and demonstrates what's possible. When the main character is ready, the teacher appears. Ethan changed the course of my life because he appeared at a time when I was ready. A complex set of circumstances were in place and the stage was set.

Your Turn: Unravelling the Shoulds and the Should-Nots

Most of us have either told someone or been told we *should* do something or we *should* be something. Often this is more about the person who is saying it than it is about the person being told. The word *should* is steeped in guilt. *You should do this or do that, or else.* Because these should statements originate with people we love or care about, not doing what we should do can leave us feeling like we have let people down or feeling like we're not enough.

Our very existence is a sign we are enough.

We are enough with our own purpose to fulfill. Let's unravel some shoulds in our life and send them from where they came.

What's a should you were told?

Fill in the Blanks:
_____ *told me I should* _____. *Today I am sending this should back to* _____.

I would like to thank _____ *for giving me this should. This should was a gift because I learned* _____ *about myself.*

Insights:
Highlight, circle, or underline thoughts from the sentence you've just written that stand out. List those thoughts below.

1.
2.
3.

Reframe:
What is a should-not you were told?
_____ *told me I should not* _____, *and today I am sending this should-not back to*

_____.

I would like to thank _____ *for giving me this should-not. This should-not was a gift because I learned* _____ *about myself.*

Insights:
Highlight, circle, or underline thoughts from the sentence you've just written that stand out. List those thoughts below.

  1.
  2.
  3.

Reframe:
Now that you have freed yourself from a should and should-not in your life, replace these with something that brings you joy.

Complete these sentences:
By letting go of this should and should-not in my life, I feel: _____.

I am going to celebrate this feeling of _____
_____ *by* _____.

Letting go of the shoulds and the should-nots can be challenging. Sometimes the shoulds and should-nots are entrenched so deeply within us, they are a part of us. Thankfully, people are put in our path at exactly the right time, so we can free ourselves from the hold the shoulds and should-nots have on us. Sometimes the universe knows before we do that we're ready to break free, and it takes someone else to make us aware.

You have two turns to delve deeper here. You now have the opportunity to journal about the people in your life who have helped you envision your world differently. The should, the should-nots, and the teachers who bring messages to you are close cousins.

Your Turn: Discovering Your Teacher, the Supposed-Tos, and the Should-Dos

Using a coloured pen of any kind, write in your journal your answers to the questions below one at a time, using your nondominant hand. Writing with the nondominant hand will feel awkward. Please persist. This simple act of writing with your nondominant hand allows you to tap into the part of the brain that is responsible for creativity and intuition. This helps to get the logical self out of the way. It's a fun exercise to try, especially if you're feeling stuck for an answer.

1. When did a teacher appear in my life?
2. What message did I receive?
3. How did this message impact my decisions?

Insights:
Circle or underline thoughts or ideas you wrote that stand out. Ideas can stand out for different reasons. It may be a recurring thought, or one you have never seen before that surprised you.

List three of those thoughts or ideas below.

1.
2.
3.

Reframe:

Reframing takes your thoughts and summarizes them in a way that speaks to you. Remember, what you write is for your eyes only.

How did this teacher contribute positively to who you are today?

Please complete these sentences:
Because this teacher came into my life, I am:

_____.

I am thankful for this teacher because I learned:

_____.

Chapter Five

You ~ The Courage to Follow Your Inner Voice

When we make decisions, we don't usually know at the time whether their impact will be large or small. Had I known the consequences my decisions would have on my life and others', I might have been afraid to choose. Having an affair wasn't the result of one decision, it was the result of many decisions. These decisions started long before I saw Ethan in the elevator.

The Ripple Effect of Your Decisions

My decision to have four children sent me down another path. I didn't arrive at the decision to have four children by chance; it was the result of growing up between Jim and Max. I was often excluded from the brother duo, so I felt alone in my family. Because of my friend Nova, I always had someone.

My goal of having four children was to protect them from my childhood pain. With four, I thought, there would always be two sets of two, with no sibling left behind. Two children didn't create enough chaos. In basketball terms, two children requires *one-on-one* defence. Move to multiples of two, and it becomes *zone* defence. Parenting with zone defence was my jam. The decisions we make are often connected to past circumstances.

I didn't anticipate my decision to have four children would be so powerful that I would ignore enormous gaps in my marriage. It took a chance meeting with a stranger to expose a void in my marriage. The encounter took on a life of its own because the timing was right; the student was ready. I found myself on a rocky, emotional journey that led me down a road of both self-discovery and enlightenment.

My oldest daughter, Reese, developed an eating disorder shortly after my marriage ended. During the long journey to recovery, I learned anorexia is about control and is often triggered by a traumatic event. The traumatic event was likely the divorce between Reese's father and me. I felt responsible for the pain all my daughters endured. I felt guilty about the choices I had made, and it has taken years to forgive myself. My unhappiness, had I stayed with their father, would have impacted my daughters negatively, and I believe this would have been even more devastating in the long run.

When Ethan came into my life, everything I thought I was and everything I thought I should be was shattered. The way we think we *should* be is based on how other people think we *should* be. If my dad had had his way, I should have been *barefoot, pregnant, and in the kitchen*. I was barefoot, pregnant, and in the kitchen for a lot of my thirties. My affair with Ethan broke my life in pieces and sent my kids and my family spiralling for a while. I rebuilt myself piece by piece, and in the process, discovered who I really was. Ethan contributed significantly to the fabric of my life and to where I am in my life today.

Eventually, my choices made my life and the lives of my children better. It's taken thirty years to say that with confidence. I endured my pain in silence. My kids have wondered why I seemed so unhappy at that time. My unhappiness came from knowing the life I had envisioned was falling apart—I was on an emotional roller coaster, and sometimes, I barely kept it together. I had lost myself in motherhood and in being a wife. It took Ethan to show me I was still a desirable woman and still my own person. I loved being a mom; however, in the early stages, it's a thankless role that includes a lot of selfless giving with little return. I lost myself in the chaos and didn't realize I had shut a part of myself down, until adversity struck.

Adversity Is a Great Teacher

The path through adversity is rich with insight. When I was at my lowest, I learned the most about myself. Falling to pieces and putting my pieces back together gave me strength. Somehow, the pieces fit differently when I got to the other side of adversity.

In this time of vulnerability, I further opened my heart to God. My faith gave me the strength to accept the choices I had made and the consequences my choices had for the people I loved. As much as my situation changed me, it changed the people around me too. When one person transforms in a group, that transformation has a ripple effect on everyone.

Some people get stuck in the *blame game*. In the short term, blaming the other person for a marriage breakdown is the easy way out. It's less painful to point fingers than it is to look within. Stu was happy to send all the blame my way, without trying to understand how he contributed to the outcome. For about a decade, he was able to persuade Reese that our marriage breakup was my fault. As a result, my relationship with Reese suffered. This is an example of the ripple effect. My actions had consequences. How Stu reacted to my actions created a whole new set of reactions that were equally destructive.

Our reaction to adversity is also a choice, and this choice can lead us down different paths. Because Stu was unable to look within himself to discover how he contributed to our marriage ending, Reese became angry and resentful. She remained stuck in this place for a long time. I'm thankful that my other three daughters didn't hold on to this level of resentment. Reese and I were able to maintain a relationship, even though at times the tension felt like another person in the room. Eventually we were all able to create a new normal.

When we were married, Stu and I co-created a family culture. After we separated, we created two very different cultures. Eve is an *old soul* who has always viewed life through an insightful lens. One day, she said, "Mom, we don't just have to pack our clothes when we go to Dad's, we have to change emotionally." That was an *aha* moment for me. I had separated from Stu because there was little emotional connection, and my daughters had a similar experience.

At Stu's house, everything remained superficial. At my house, I wanted to know how everyone was feeling. As the girls became older, they were able to see our differences. At one point, Kendra asked, "Mom, how did you marry Dad?" Kendra understood how different we were and gave me confirmation I had done the right thing.

My kids continue to have a great relationship with their dad. Stu and I are happier apart than we could have been together, and the girls see that now. Listening to and acting on my inner voice took strength and every bit of courage I could muster.

Trusting my inner voice and getting to the other side of adversity had transformational powers and brought me closer to who I am meant to be. Adversity was God's vehicle for change.

I promised myself I would write a book when I had a life-changing spiritual experience. Since then, I have learned to trust my inner voice. My voice within has been a beacon of inspiration and encouragement as well as my guiding light.

Listening to the Voice Within

I had just been given two very different job offers: one in recruitment, similar to what I had been doing for about two years, and one selling an assessment tool I was passionate about.

On the surface, a career decision isn't a life-changing choice. I knew I could always reverse and redirect if I had made the wrong choice. This was one of those small but mighty choices that packed a punch.

Although I enjoyed being a recruiter, I was working for an entrepreneur who was extremely difficult. One minute she would be engaging and supportive, and the next minute, her mood would flip. Without warning she would become a ranting, angry person with deep-seated rage targeted at me. No matter how hard I worked, my best was never good enough. She would ultimately find fault in everything I did.

One day, I received a call from someone I met briefly who had known this entrepreneur for a long time. She called to let me know someone in her network was wanting to hire a recruiter. I took this phone call as a sign it was time to explore what else was available in the job market. I had spent too many nights in tears wondering what I had done to trigger the entrepreneur's irrational outbursts.

People don't leave jobs; they leave leaders. Once I decided it was time to leave, I received those two job offers. I felt like I was at a fork in the road. One job would keep me on my current career path, and the other would take me in a completely new direction. A friend suggested I take a break from the city to enjoy the tranquility and gain clarity, and the right decision would present itself. Rox, my labradoodle, and I jumped on a ferry and headed out of the city to discover my best path forward.

The first morning, I dreamt I was in my dad's office. My dad had been gone for about ten years, and it felt like he showed up in the dream to guide me to the right decision. In my dream, I was sitting behind his desk, cold-calling, and in the next moment I was dancing with my dad. We weren't following rigid steps, we were magically swirling around without a care in the world, having fun and laughing. I remember waking up, thinking how vivid and real my dream felt. That dream was meant to prepare me for what happened next.

Before anyone else was awake, Rox and I went for a walk. We were on Gambier, a Gulf Island in the Pacific Ocean in British Columbia, Canada. Gambier is a magical place, covered with rain forest. The foliage is lush and green. Moss hangs ornately from the trees, and the fresh air is crisp and restorative. I was at peace with my pooch. She happily bounded through the forest in silence, and I was with only my thoughts. I remember praying, asking God for direction. Suddenly, I heard a voice from within, loudly and clearly. This voice simply asked me a question:

What makes you dance?

Immediately, I had my answer. I decided to join the assessment company. I rushed back to tell my friend. A few hours later, over lunch and a glass of wine, I had a sinking feeling. I thought: *Oh no, dancing with my girls in the kitchen brings me joy and makes me dance. To be able to afford the house we're in, I needed to choose recruitment.*

Our house had provided my girls and me a safe place to live—a sense of belonging and stability within a thriving community. My mom wrote a large cheque, no questions asked, and trusted me to keep her investment safe by keeping the roof she provided over our heads. This is an enormous responsibility and a gift that has kept on giving. I chose to honour my mom's generosity, unconditional love, and unwavering trust, and stayed in recruitment so I could afford the house my mom so generously afforded my girls and me.

Dancing with my dad in my dream prepared me to answer confidently the question God asked from within. In my dream, dancing with my dad was joyful, carefree, and grounded in love. I see now that God was asking me this question so I would choose the path that would bring more joy, fun, and love into my life. In the same dream, I had dreamt of cold-calling behind my dad's desk, and it was my cold-calling ability that opened the doors to both opportunities.

Messages Sent to Guide You

I was ready to receive and trust a powerful message that day. This message led me to where I was supposed to be.

God gave us free choice, and with that, life presents many twists and turns. Sometimes a leap of faith is all we have. Every decision we make leads us somewhere. Often, we don't know where that somewhere is until we arrive. It took years before I could put the pieces together.

When faced with two career options, I had to choose. I ended up choosing the more difficult option. It was difficult because of my perspective. I was fearful of getting into another situation in which the entrepreneurs who owned the business would be as emotionally volatile as the person I had been reporting to. I had difficulty differentiating the role of recruiter from the situation and hoped not all entrepreneurs were as challenging. I took a leap of faith, and my life changed for the better.

Your Turn: Trusting Your Inner Voice

With all the demands, the noise, chaos, and distractions, the inner voice is sometimes unheard and overshadowed. Journaling has a magical way of connecting us with our inner voice. Find a quiet place to journal, preferably at the beginning of the day, before the rest of the world is awake, or at the end of the day, as you unwind. The best time to journal is a personal choice. You will discover when ideas flow most easily and when you are at your best. We are all individuals.

A quiet space and consistent routine signal the mind it is time to relax. When I was writing this book, I would go to the same room in the morning and begin by lighting three candles and saying a prayer. Most mornings the thoughts would flow through me. I trained my mind to shift into a relaxed state that allowed my inner voice to be heard. This approach applies to journaling. Remember to write freely, without judgment. This is not a time to edit your words, this is your time to be curious about yourself and gain insight from within.

When I use coloured markers to describe something, my thoughts flow more easily. It's like I am expressing myself as a child again. When I was growing up, we called them *magic markers*, and there is truth in that name. Let your thoughts flow onto paper with magic markers and feel like a child again.

Writing with magic markers, describe a time you trusted your inner voice.

What happened when you trusted your inner voice?

Circle, underline, or highlight words and phrases that speak your truth.

You may have written ideas you have had in the back of your mind for a long time but had received no attention. Putting these thoughts on paper will bring them to the forefront of your mind and bring them into the light. Putting thoughts on paper makes them real. Please list your insights on the next page.

Insights:
    1.
    2.
    3.

Reframe:
What kernels of wisdom do you gain from the insights you have listed?

Please complete this sentence:
*My inner voice is:*_____.

Learning to listen to the voice within is like learning to use a new muscle; it takes practice. Look at your list of insights and describe your inner voice and why you have the confidence to listen to it, really hear it, and take action.

I trust my inner voice because: _____.

Chapter Six

Roles ~ Who You Are in the World

Every job we have contributes to molding us in into who we are. At age fifteen, I worked in a veterinary clinic. Every day before school, I would jump on my bike to arrive at the back door of the clinic, located off a dark alley. I arrived long before the doctors every morning to check on the animals and clean the cages. When the doctors arrived, I would assist with treating the animals back to health.

I would walk through the door, not knowing what I would find. Some animals were boarders, but most of the animals were patients. Sometimes animals wouldn't make it through the night, and it was my job to remove their cold, rigour-mortis-stiffened bodies. Being an animal lover, I found this difficult, especially when my job was to put the bodies of someone's beloved pet into a deep freezer along with many other frozen corpses.

One day I arrived to find a stranger lying on the green garbage bags in the back shed. I rushed past the motionless body and quickly locked the door behind me. By the time the veterinarians arrived, the person was gone, leaving only an indentation of his body on the bags. These doctors—both men—didn't believe me and dismissed this mysterious stranger as being a part of my imagination. I worked for two veterinarians who gave me adult responsibilities and then treated me like a child when I shared a story outside their comfort zone.

Not being believed was the most disturbing part of this story. This experience fuels my fire within to help women find their voice, be valued, and taken seriously. Decades later, I still picture that person lying there and remember wondering if he was dead.

Another time, I arrived to find the clinic totally ransacked. The contents of the cabinets were emptied, and there were pills strewn all over the floor. Someone had broken in during the night, and I was the first to arrive on the scene. The doctors didn't dispute this reality.

Work Experiences Shape You

Work experiences during the formative high school years and the memories of them have a lasting impact and are woven into the fabric of our lives. They, like our high school experiences, build the foundation for what lies ahead. These experiences weave their way into the soul of our being. Experiences in our impressionable years stay with us and shape us.

This job contributed to my sense of courage and resiliency. At a young age, I was faced with situations that were beyond my years, and I learned to cope in the moment. Nothing had prepared me for my experiences or for my emotions. I remember holding a very sick puppy as he was put to sleep. His little body went limp in my hands. Taking that little pooch from his loving owners and holding him while I walked to the back room to end his life is an experience that stays with me.

I saw the best and the worst in people. Some people do not deserve the privilege of owning pets. I saw horrific results of pet owners' neglect. When I see an animal tied up outside alone and vulnerable or left in a car on a hot day or being pulled on a leash alongside a bike, forced to run while the owner is riding, I want to scream.

While I was working at the animal clinic, I held another job at a venereal disease clinic. The VD clinic was located close to my high school, so I would see fellow students visit the clinic. I don't remember anyone stressing I should maintain confidentiality. After coming close to losing Nova because I shared her secret, no one had to stress the importance of confidentiality. My previous experience with adversity taught me lessons that contributed to my growth and success in this role.

Our work experiences build upon one another and are meant to teach us lessons. These lessons become a part of the foundation that guides us throughout our lives.

Experiencing setbacks and hurdles in work serves a purpose. If your work life were a smooth ride, you would be robbed of the opportunity to discover yourself and to tap into your internal sense of purpose.

The Golf Ball and the Stadium

God intentionally makes our life journey difficult to connect us to our faith and our faith journey. In the process, we move closer to our purpose and experience a sense of wonder when we discover it. Similar to peeling back the layers of an onion, we get closer to what is truly in our heart. Just like a computer, we draw from files we have stored in our brains. Years ago, I met with a psychiatrist whose name escapes me. He told me something that stuck with me. He said the conscious part of our brain is the size of a golf ball. The subconscious part of the brain—all the stuff we have filed away—is the size of a stadium.

In other words, the conscious side of our brain includes our conscious thoughts, thoughts we are aware of having. We can tell the conscious side of the brain to stop thinking about something, to turn away, to not let something in. The subconscious side of the brain takes everything in, whether we want it to or not. Our subconscious is taking in every noise, noting every movement of every person we meet, keeping track of all our surroundings. The subconscious mind never sleeps, keeping us alive and safe. If you have ever fallen asleep while watching TV and had a dream integrating the show you are watching, you know what I mean. Our subconscious mind is watching, integrating, and staying active while our conscious mind is taking a break, getting ready to tackle another day.

Making my decision to stay in recruitment was the result of several complex factors. These factors went beyond facing my fear of working for entrepreneurs. I drew on experiences and memories that happened long before I made my decision.

We draw from our subconscious; we integrate past experiences and past comments into our own truth. Decisions based on our past shape our future. Once I understood the past influences that impacted my current decisions, I was able to make conscious decisions that served me better. This was a process of self-reflection and self-discovery. It took time journaling and working with a counsellor to uncover the files in my subconscious. It's like following a thread of decisions that lead us to a place. When these decisions are conscious, they lead us where we want to be instead of somewhere random.

Our work experience is rich with lessons when we're open to receiving them. Soon after university, I was working at an employment center for students and received a very painful and life-changing lesson. This was my first leadership role as a supervisor. Up to this point, I had relied on myself to achieve goals. This changed when I became the leader; I had to rely on others to achieve goals, and this was difficult. My only role model of a leader was my dad. Employees at his office, except for people who worked closely with him, were afraid of him. I had observed this during the summers I had worked for him. The person he portrayed at the office was different from the person he was at home.

I observed my father's leadership style, and it appeared as if part of him liked people being afraid of him because that meant he could do his own work. There was no such thing as an open-door policy with my dad; that door was shut! One day at the center, sitting in my office all alone, the way my dad preferred to work, I had the impression that everyone was slacking off. This was something I had no tolerance for and went out to the front office in a rage. The team was shocked and dumbfounded by my behaviour. I was surprised and embarrassed by my own behaviour.

The next day I spoke calmly with each team member and apologized. Each person was able to express their feelings, and we seemed to move forward—everyone but me. On the evening we were scheduled to celebrate an end-of-summer party, someone broke into my car. I used this as an excuse to avoid the party. The team talked to me on the phone to express how much they wanted me there, but I couldn't bring myself to go.

That experience taught me many things about myself. I realized I'm not my dad, and my leadership style is different. I would much rather be among the team doing the work and having fun, not stuck away by myself in an office. It's a challenge to forgive myself when I make a mistake, and I have trouble letting things go. As I reflect, it's clear I haven't completely let this experience go. We are all works in progress.

Roles and Responsibilities: We All Show Up as the Full Package

We bring our childhood experiences, traumas, sibling rivalries, and homelife to the workplace. That old expression to *leave the baggage at the door* makes sense in theory, but in reality, it rarely happens. The subconscious sneaks in, just like it did for me at the employment center. Sometimes, we don't anticipate how we will react in certain situations. Painful experiences help us become more aware the next time we are faced with similar situations.

I gravitate toward people at work who remind me of my brothers and other important people in my life. Life presents endless opportunities to learn about ourselves. When I am consciously open to the possibility that relationships don't just *happen*, they are part of a greater plan, I am able to regard a situation with curiosity instead of judgment.

One of my favourite work experiences was early in my career. Several people had been let go from manufacturing jobs. The community college I worked for received government funding to train and prepare these people to return to the workforce. At twenty-five, newly married, I facilitated thirty students ages eighteen through sixty-five with this transition. It was my job to help these students write a cover letter and resume and to prepare for interviews. Because of the diverse ages, the conversation was lively and fun. Together we laughed lots and grew from one another.

After my humbling and painful leadership experience at the employment center, this position helped me regain my confidence. This role came into my life for a reason, not a lifetime. This role was a highlight in my career, and this experience brought me joy and put me on a path toward a career I am passionate about.

My dad had always told me "Those who can, do. Those who can't, teach." Even though I loved this role, his voice stopped me from pursuing this type of work.

I don't agree with my dad's perspective about teachers. Teachers create lasting memories for many of us. Lessons learned from teachers impact career decisions and inspire people throughout their lives. I have heard many stories throughout my recruitment career of teachers and the positive influence they've had on individuals.

The choice to take another path in my career was influenced by my dad's beliefs. At the time I took these beliefs on as my own. I know now that I needed to have that positive experience to better understand my leadership style. I discovered how much I enjoyed being a part of the group doing the work: striving, growing, celebrating wins, laughing, and having fun together on the journey. This experience was a necessary steppingstone in my career and in my personal development.

Your Turn: Work Experiences in the Impressionable Years

Think about a work experience you had in your impressionable years. This time, we will connect with your thoughts and ideas by creating a *mind map*. A mind map is a visual way of organizing your thoughts. Similar to journaling, mind mapping can provide insight. Mind mapping brings thoughts that may be swirling in your mind or hidden within from the darkness into the light. It will help you see the big picture and identify connections you may not have otherwise noticed. The process of creating a mind map can be therapeutic in itself.

Open your journal to a blank page. Using a magic marker, write down an early work experience in the middle of the page and draw a circle around it; this is the *core concept*. From this circle, draw branches. On these branches, write ideas about how this early work experience is connected to your thoughts and behaviours today. For example, the branches could say LESSONS LEARNED, WHAT I LEARNED ABOUT MYSELF, WHAT I LEARNED ABOUT OTHERS, LESSONS I HAVE LEARNED TO LET GO. From each of these branches, draw secondary branches and go a little deeper in your thoughts. On the branch that says WHAT I LEARNED ABOUT OTHERS, create a new branch for everything you learned about people during that one work experience.

Circle or highlight words or phrases that still apply to you today. These phrases could represent thoughts that continue to show up in your life, or they can represent challenges you have overcome. Write these highlighted words and phrases in your journal. Use many colours when you are creating your mind map. It's meant to be a fun exercise that can inspire creative thought, connecting your past work experience and who you are in the world today.

Do your best to put your ideas down on paper without overthinking. Let the ideas flow. The goal is to transfer the ideas floating around in your head to paper. Little seeds of wisdom and insight are within all of us. Bring these seeds into the light so they can continue to grow and flourish.

These steps may help you get started:

1. Create a mind map of an early work experience.
2. Circle some insights that stand out in your mind map.
3. How does this early work experience contribute to who you are today?

Insights:
1.
2.
3.

Reframe:
From the list of insights, write a sentence about how this early work experience contributes to who you are today in the world.

This early work experience taught me:

_____.

These lessons show up for me today when:

_____.

Your Five Favourite Roles

Start with a new page in your journal. Across the top of the page, write five favourite roles you are or have fulfilled in your life so far. These are favourite roles for a reason. My goal is to help you uncover why these roles are your favourites.

Under each role, list all the responsibilities you fulfill.

After you have completed the list, circle your favourite responsibilities from each column. Write the words below.

Look for commonalities. Is there a common thread? Are there themes that keep appearing in these roles?

List three responsibilities that stand out. What makes these roles special?

Insights:

    1.

    2.

    3.

Reframe:

We do our best work in the world when we enjoy what we do. When we enjoy what we're doing, the people who are with us benefit too. When we enjoy what we are doing, we create a positive ripple effect that affects others in a positive way. Please complete the sentence below.

*I am happiest when:*_____.

Chapter Seven

Seeing Yourself Through Others

In each compartment of life—such as health, wealth, work, relationships, and spirituality—we are where we are in each area because of the choices we have made. Choices are influenced by past experiences, relationships, chance meetings, or comments people make. A family member, a teacher, a friend, or a colleague can make a comment that sticks with us and influences future decisions. We often aren't conscious how a comment or experience is influencing our decisions because it's lost in the vast stadium of our subconscious.

When I took my decision-making off autopilot, I started making choices that served me and brought me closer to who I was meant to be rather than the person I thought I should be.

While my mom very generously provided the means to buy a house that has given stability to my family, over the years, the house has required maintenance, and unexpected expenses have occurred.

My mom had expressed concern and anxiety about my ability to manage this responsibility on my own. Soon after the house was purchased, she wondered how I would cope when something inevitably broke down. I gained enormous clarity during this conversation. In the past, I would have become anxious too. On this occasion, I was able to listen to my mom from a different vantage point. Part of me was smiling, nodding, and listening to all my mom's fears, and another part of me was discovering where my voices of scarcity and fear originated. This conversation helped me gain perspective.

As my mom spoke, I thought: *I will find a way.* Today, I still catch myself going into scarcity mode because doubts are always lurking in the background, waiting for a crack to emerge. My fear was more about my mom's perspective than it was about mine. My mom was raised by parents who survived the great depression, and she was passing down lessons she learned in her childhood. When I discovered the origin of my fear, I was able to recognize the fear for what it was and let it go. Instead of holding on to fear and being paralyzed by it, I acknowledged its existence and let it wash over me and dissipate in order to keep moving forward.

We have the choice to either take on these secondhand experiences as our own or recognize their source and set them free. Some lessons from our parents will serve us, and some won't. By unravelling where our voices originate, we can better understand the decisions we make in all compartments of our lives. I have stopped taking these voices at face value. I look below the surface and wonder if there is something I can learn, or if there is something I need to let go of in order to grow.

When I worked at my dad's office and observed how afraid people were of my dad, this gave me insight. I wondered how this intimidating man could be the same guy I knew at home.

As his daughter, I saw beyond this tough exterior into the *mush-ball* within. I saw my dad as a father who was trying to figure out how to be a parent. Losing both his parents at nineteen and being an only child, he had very little to draw from.

In business, I discovered there is a whole world of people who are playing the role of someone they believe they are supposed to be, and on the inside, they are someone else. When cold-calling potential clients, I looked for the person behind the façade. Although the stories were different, every person I called, usually men, had this inner mush-ball, and it was my job to find it. I would say something unexpected, tap into their sense of humour, and throw them off their game. In a split-second, their response gave me a glimpse into who they really were. I was able to assess people's personality styles and adapt my style to align with theirs.

I wish my dad had lived long enough for me to share this with him; he would have been surprised by how much I learned through observation.

The Origin of Your Values

Soon after I started working with another recruitment company, I knew I had made the right decision. Volatile mood swings, erratic behaviour, and teary nights were gone. I finally fit in and felt like I belonged. Fit is based on values. If values in any relationship aren't aligned, the relationships eventually end. It's simple and complex at the same time. Family, friends, and experiences influence our values. For example, as a result of the lessons from my breach of confidence with Nova, my values now include being trustworthy and maintaining confidences.

Our values begin forming when we are young. Experiences in our impressionable years spark our value formation. I was unkind to a classmate in high school. That experience hurt and scarred her and helped me learn to embrace and celebrate people's differences.

My dad told me all women should be "barefoot pregnant and in the kitchen." One of my values is to voice my opinion and let my feelings be known when I don't agree with something.

Values don't just happen; they morph within us over time. I picture our values as these little seeds that sprout and eventually turn into wise old trees. Our values are firmly in place, taking root and growing within us long before we are aware. Our personal values really come to light when they don't match the values of other people.

When this happens, sometimes I feel uneasy in the pit of my stomach, or I hear a tiny voice in my head telling me something isn't right. My values are telling me to pay attention: Something, or someone, doesn't fit or align with who I am. This voice becomes louder. It can even be apparent in the form of health issues, until we make some changes. The word *disease*, when broken into syllables, is *dis*-ease. Dis-ease is what we feel when our values are out of alignment, and sometimes, disease is how our bodies let us know. Our bodies are wise and scream out in different ways to make us pay attention when something is off track.

Your Turn: Roles ~ Responsibilities and Values Alignment

Refer to your list of Roles and Responsibilities. Re-list your five favourite roles in your life:

1.
2.
3.
4.
5.

Now, list the responsibility that aligns with each role.

1.
2.
3.
4.
5.

Look at the List of Values in the box below. Choose a value from the list that aligns with each role and responsibility and write it in your journal.

	Role	Responsibility	Values Match
1			
2			
3			
4			
5			

List of Values

Courage	Respect	Continuous Learning
Fun	Love	Loyalty
Leadership	Contribution	Inner Peace
Happiness	Honesty	Competence
Achievement	Compassion	Justice
Creativity	Recognition	Adventure
Freedom	Reputation	Personal
Service	Friendship	Development
Work Ethic	Authenticity	Wealth
Faith	Kindness	Add your own:
Meaningful Work	Family	

List five values that are core to who you are:

1.

2.

3.

4.

5.

Insights:
Write an observation about each value and how it shows up in your life. For example, do your values show up for you in order of importance, or are they all equally important? How do you feel when one of your values is missing from what you're doing, or in the person you're with?

1.
2.
3.
4.
5.

Reframe:
Review your list of values combined with your observations. Write a sentence describing how these values show up in your life, using present tense.

Please complete this sentence:
I must have: _____.

Your Turn: Roles and Responsibilities ~ Dig Deeper

Choose one responsibility from your list above and describe it in your journal. How do you feel when you are fulfilling this role and responsibility? Look at your five core values. Choose the value this role and responsibility represents. Write about this value as it relates to this role and responsibility following the prompts below:

Please describe your responsibility.

How do you feel when you are fulfilling this responsibility?

From your list of values, what value does this responsibility represent?

Why is the value _____ core to who you are? Please explain. Answer this same question for each of your top five values.

Insights:
    1.
    2.
    3.

Reframe:

Highlight or circle key phrases in the words that you wrote. Write these words and phrases in a sentence that is meaningful for you: _____

Chapter Eight

The State of Flow ~ When Time Stands Still

Recognized and named by psychologist Mihaly Csikszentmihalyi, *Flow Theory* describes the state of being when we focus on something, and hours feel like minutes as we complete a task or activity. When I first got to know Beau and began falling in love with him, *flow* was the perfect term for how it felt. Although there were challenges, it all seemed to fit and felt to be a part of something bigger.

Flow isn't something that is recognized all at once; it's a journey. Much like when you discover an activity that brings you joy—perhaps it's a sport, walking through a museum, painting a picture, whatever it is—there is a feeling that's different from how you feel when you're doing other activities. You need to have experienced other activities that don't evoke the same feeling to know what flow is. Once you have experienced this feeling, you want more of it.

Doing what gives us that sense of flow is often accompanied with doing something that is just outside our comfort zone. Reaching outside our comfort zone causes us to push ourselves in ways we may not have before. This takes time and courage. The feeling of flow is something we strive to have more of in our life. It's also something we earn over time. The state of flow is a sign you're moving toward understanding what makes you dance.

Soon after I started working at the recruitment firm, the number of employees increased, and we outgrew the space we were in. I found myself sharing an office with Beau, one of the partners who hired me. We were both responsible for cold-calling and bringing in new business, so it made sense for us to work collaboratively. One day, Beau said something on the phone that made me smile. But more to my surprise and horror, I realized in that moment I was attracted to him. It was a sinking feeling. I had no idea about Beau's home situation. I felt an attraction, and we were working only three feet apart.

I was long out of my marriage. I was dating someone I had been trying to break up with for two years. The relationship was no longer working, yet every time I tried to break it off, he would find a way back, and I let it happen.

Beau and I worked well together. Soon a friendship began to develop. Working with someone in such close quarters, there is nothing to hide. Beau's kids would call, and I would hear every interaction. We would share parenting stories and stories about our pets. We celebrated business wins and grew from our losses. We had fun and we learned from each other.

With four daughters ages fifteen and under, I would arrive at the office at 8:30 feeling like I had already put in a day's work. Mornings were hectic and getting kids—including two teenagers with attitude—off to school was exhausting. Breakfasts and lunches, pets fed and walked, sibling fights, teenage drama—I often wonder how I survived those years. To add to the chaos, I decided to get a puppy—Rox.

Our family had lost our first dog, Morgie, and I didn't want the kids growing up feeling they missed out on getting another dog because their parents divorced. My cousin Sam, a retired veterinarian, suggested we get a labradoodle. A labradoodle had the right temperament to fit our household where chaos and constant activity was the norm. My friends at work helped me source a person who bred these dogs who were so new, it was the first time I had heard of the breed. Rox was one of the originals.

When it came time to spay Rox, I was referred to a veterinarian who came highly recommended. To close the surgical opening, they used a gel in place of stitches for the first time. It resulted in dissolving Rox's skin instead of healing it. My experience working in a vet clinic proved invaluable as I treated Rox every day to heal her underbelly. I had to stay home with her one day to ensure she wasn't causing additional damage to the wound. I phoned Beau, and he immediately suggested I sneak Rox up the back stairs into the office, so I could keep an eye on her. That's what I did, and Rox slept safely and happily under our desks. This experience further cemented my friendship with Beau.

I knew Beau was married, and that's all I knew. He was my work friend. The only time I saw him outside of work was at company get-togethers. I enjoyed most of the people within the firm, but I was aware that when Beau left these events early, I was disappointed to see him leave.

He rarely talked about his spouse, and she never came into the office. I later found out their marriage had been on-again, off-again, for years. Beau came into work one day and seemed different—lighter, like the weight of the world had been lifted. I noticed he was not wearing his wedding ring. That was a happy day.

Six months went by, and nothing was mentioned. Beau started dating. Our friendship remained natural and genuine. Not able to decide for himself, Beau brought in a suit and two ties and asked which one was better to wear on his date. He trusted my fashion sense and asked for my opinion.

I had finally broken up for good with the person I was dating. Beau would kid me about how I didn't break up very well. Eventually, I did the millennial thing and broke up over text. On a snowy cold day, I had just finished a meeting with a potential client. Beau phoned to hear how it went, although Beau's real reason for calling was to ask me out to meet his hockey buddies. Beau played professional hockey and often talked about his hockey friends, so I said yes to an evening outside of work.

For six months, Beau had been living with his daughter and son-in-law. I persuaded him to move to the city to experience something new. He took my advice and was finishing up his second week living on his own in a trendy, gentrifying area of Vancouver. Beau had become the envy of his friends. Not only was he single, but he was also living downtown, free to make his own decisions and live life on his terms.

I remember asking my wise daughter Eve "How can I be with someone who signs my pay cheques?" She said, matter-of-factly, "Mom, how do you know you're *not* supposed to be with Beau?" That answer shook me a little. Eve was right; how did I know?

So when Beau called that day to ask me to meet his hockey buddies, I immediately said yes.

Stars Align When Values Align

This was the first time we were outside the work environment without our work teammates. Mix that with a little wine, and it wasn't long before we were on the dance floor, holding hands. I'm thankful Beau's friends pointed out the obvious and for that glass of wine that gave me the courage to kiss Beau on the cheek. He turned his head at the perfect moment, and instead of kissing his cheek, I kissed Beau's ear. Oh well; the delivery wasn't there, but the message was received loudly and clearly.

The legendary "big-city Beau" was fleeting. Beau's friends remind us of that every chance they get. That night changed the course of our lives forever and set us both spinning. The first feeling of love was like a drug for me. It muddled my thinking. One minute I was elated with joy, and the next minute I was fearful of what this would mean for our future. We had crossed the HR rule. Employees in love: working together is one thing; the owner of the company in love with a direct report is more complicated.

For the next few weeks, we continued working as usual. Up to this point, we had only confirmed there was an attraction, something Beau could no longer ignore.

We decided to go out again on another Friday night, to see if we enjoyed being together socially. That experiment was a success. Beau and I talked for hours in this crowded bar, and it felt like no one else existed. One of Beau's hockey friends was with us at the beginning of the evening. He still jokes when he sees us today. He left for an intramural hockey game. Hours went by, yet these hours seemed like minutes. We spent the entire time rapt in conversation. When Beau's friend returned, I asked—because I obviously wasn't thinking straight—where he had gone. He replied, "just to the bathroom." We were in our own little world.

Beau asked if I would like to join him again the third Friday. I was like a school kid. Eve had put a couple of clothing options out on my bed. Eve saw me in a whole new light, and I think she is still scarred to this day. I couldn't decide what to wear and nothing was right. At one point, I remember saying, "That's it; I'm not going." I was like a teenager. I was usually the one making all the decisions, and that evening, I couldn't make the simplest one. Finally, Eve coaxed me back to sanity, and I went out and had the most memorable night of my life. I could have been wearing a green garbage bag and Beau wouldn't have cared. He was happy I was there.

We met with a few friends, and at last, we were alone. We were sitting in a circular booth, located in a restaurant and bar. The restaurant was filled with people and the noise was through the roof. We were happy in our little space, away from the crowds in a world all our own. Then it happened: Beau kissed me. Here we were, me in my late forties, Beau in his late fifties, and we were like a couple of high school kids.

Hours flew by like minutes, and when we finally became aware of our surroundings, the patrons had all gone, and all the chairs were up on the tables. I wondered what the employees thought. Not once did anyone come near us. We were an island unto ourselves in this busy place located in the heart of the city, *making out* for all the world to see.

The employees must have been relieved when we finally acknowledged their presence. I'm thankful to those considerate people. That was the most magical evening. The world could have come crumbling down around us, and we wouldn't have noticed. I remember the shock on the manager's face when I asked if he could please order two cabs.

We could no longer deny what was happening. We needed to make some decisions. We needed to be honest with Beau's business partner and the rest of the team. To strategize next steps, Beau and I decided to meet at my place, this time with no wine. Beau arrived and we ordered sushi. When the sushi guy arrived, Rox escaped. Rox was an active puppy and an exuberant escape artist. She saw her opening, and without us noticing, Rox was off on an adventure.

Just as we were getting out the sushi, I noticed Rox was gone. It was pouring rain. Beau started walking the streets, calling Rox's name. I jumped in the car and started combing the neighbourhood. My house is surrounded by busy streets. Anything could have happened. Beau found Rox first. I remember sitting in my dry, warm car seeing Beau in the pouring rain with his hand on Rox's collar, walking across the street, soaking wet. That night ticked another big box for me. Beau loved animals and would do what he had to do to keep our four-legged friends safe.

Your Turn: Discover What Flow Means to You

In flow, we become so engrossed in what we are doing, we lose our sense of time, and what we are doing brings us great joy and satisfaction. The story I shared above is an exaggerated example of flow, meant to demonstrate how powerful the state of flow can be.

In your journal, describe a time when you were in flow and how it felt.

What core value did this experience represent?

How would you feel if you were able to experience a flow state in your life every day?

Insights:

Highlight or circle key phrases in the words you wrote.

1.
2.
3.

Reframe:

Put your list of phrases or words from your insights into a sentence that is meaningful for you:

_____

Please complete these sentences:

When I am in flow I feel: _____.

I know I am living my truth when: _____.

Chapter Nine

Together in Adversity

With adversity comes change, and this change takes on many forms. Adversity can move us forward and change who we were before it came into our lives, or adversity can keep us stuck in one place, paralyzed with fear of what's next. This fear can turn to feelings of anger and blame for being in what feels like a helpless state. Adversity flows toward us, and we stand still to steady ourself, protect ourself from a wave of pain or fear of the unknown. Eventually that feeling dissipates, and we are able to take one step forward. One step at a time we can become unstuck.

That's the situation we faced after we revealed to Beau's business partner and our team that we were in a relationship. Questions of favoritism surfaced. His partner eventually left. This can happen when a third person enters and influences decisions made within the partnership.

Beau invested a lot of money into office renovations, and the other partner had no skin in the game. He was the ideas guy, and ideas cost money—a lot of it. This was 2007, right before the economic downturn. With recruitment being a leading indicator of the economy, business stopped overnight. No one was hiring. People were scared and were letting employees go.

It was the perfect storm. Beau's partnership crumbled and so did the business. One night I woke up with a start, wondering how we could pay the bills. Money stopped and the bills kept coming. At three in the morning, we came to the realization something drastic had to be done because we couldn't pay the office rent.

The next day, Beau went into the office and started packing boxes. Beau's business partner was nowhere to be found. There is a popular saying about business that has never made sense to me: *It's business; it's not personal.* Business is very personal, and the pain goes right to the core.

The office we left behind was newly renovated and highly sought after. The leasing company was able to rent our office space the following month. This was the beginning of a very difficult chapter.

Everyone in the office was let go. A staff of fifteen people was downsized to two. Beau and I had put all our hopes and dreams into one company. We didn't anticipate a global financial crisis and economic meltdown. When the market crashed, we only had ourselves to rely on. We didn't have the backing of a large corporation to lessen the blow. We had to withstand the hit and do everything in our power to pick ourselves up, dust ourselves off, and keep moving forward.

Even in that time of turmoil, an unexpected bright light appeared and showed us the way. We had one client who saw the financial crisis as an opportunity. To keep the roof over our heads, I went to work for this client, utilizing my cold-calling skills to raise institutional capital.

Beau continued to search for talent, and he built this client's leadership team. He supported this client from the outside, and I worked with this same client from within. All was well for almost two years. In the end, the owners made some strategic errors and the company shut down. It was a sad day for many when this business ceased to exist. Business is very personal.

Adversity on the Road to Self-Awareness

I ended up rejoining Beau's recruitment company. The world was slowly bouncing back from the economic crash, and we were back in business. Being inside a company for two years taught me a lot. Although it was a relief to receive a steady pay cheque, the experience confirmed I was better aligned with being in my own business. I came back to recruitment with a better understanding of how leaders influence culture.

When I returned, it was a very different place. We were now a company with three people, and I found myself in a group of three, with two men.

The other guy wasn't happy I was returning; adding a third shifted the power dynamic.

The last time I had encountered this situation, the first guy left and so did the next. I take responsibility. I realize I have little tolerance for mediocrity. In a way, it was a replay of my student employment center experience. I was older, not quite as impulsive, and the driving force was the same. When people's work ethic is misaligned with mine, I'm unable to remain silent. Strong work ethic is a value that goes to my core.

Both my parents would tell my brothers and me to "be the best we could be" every day. This value appears when I encounter situations in which I feel people aren't giving their best. My intolerance for mediocrity is a strength until it becomes out of balance. Any strength becomes a weakness when it's allowed to run wild.

I have learned to surround myself with people who share the value of bringing their best. I still struggle with people who aren't as driven or as passionate as I am. To balance my struggle, I try to uncover what motivates an individual. Everyone is passionate about something. I ask questions to discover the passion within, and this helps me be more compassionate, understanding, and less judgmental. It took me a long time to connect the dots and understand where my values originated.

Should we want to change our behaviour, change requires self-awareness, acceptance, and forgiveness. Self-awareness starts by examining the past a little bit at a time. If your life were a piece of fabric woven together with all its intricacies, it would be much like unravelling one thread at a time to reveal and rediscover parts of your life that are always there—a part of you, waiting to be discovered.

I have had to forgive myself a lot over the years. Forgiveness starts with the knowledge that something needs to shift. Although we are a product of our parents, we don't have to continue our parents' old patterns. Shifting behaviour takes courage and acceptance—courage to look within and the acceptance a behaviour no longer serves us. Over the years, I began to forgive myself for some of my behaviours. I also had to accept and forgive my parents for theirs.

Growing Through Adversity

Executive recruitment is a very competitive business with no barrier to entry. Anyone can say they are a *headhunter*. Being in this profession doesn't require extra education or a designation. The value of any recruiter is in the results. My goal was to differentiate us from the rest of the companies within our industry. Although it took longer than expected, we became well known in the industry.

Beau and I have spent twenty-four hours together every day for more than eighteen years. People wonder how we do it. It's easy because together, we are in flow. Our values in every aspect of our lives are aligned. Our commitment to our work and our strong work ethic is similar. I don't have to question if Beau is working hard; he is, relentlessly, especially when work is difficult. Our family values also align. We have a truly blended family with seven children. Our seven have partners who feel like our children too. We have a growing number of grandchildren who are all different with minds of their own.

About ten years ago, I became Beau's business partner. Beau had jokingly referred to me as his "silent partner." This made me smile; we both knew I was rarely silent.

Maybe it's an occupational hazard, but I can quickly unravel other people's stories to understand who they are. By asking questions, I'm able to get a picture of people's perspectives. I gain insight into the experiences and expectations that have contributed to making them the person they are.

My daughter-in-law Jade was raised in Eastern Europe. She remembers the day the Berlin Wall went down. One day she was living in a communist country, and the next day she wasn't. Sometimes I see glimmers of the impact growing up under communist rule has had on Jade. One of many things I admire about her is her courage to go against traditional ways of thinking. She speaks out if something doesn't make sense. She doesn't accept status quo and will question things I accept without asking why. Through listening and trying to understand Jade's perspective, I am forced to get out of my comfort zone and find myself questioning too.

For example, processed food has no place in Jade's household because food manufacturers are all about profit and are not to be trusted as having our best interests at heart. Jade also questions the motives behind pharmaceutical companies, large corporations, and government, to name a few. I tend to be much more trusting of large companies and institutions. Jade has opened my eyes to ask more questions and be more curious about what's happening around us. She believes situations and outcomes are not always what they seem. Jade and I learn and grow from our different perspectives, and because our values align, we all work well together. We see the world differently because of the vast differences between our perspectives growing up in Canada and growing up in Czechoslovakia under communist rule.

The simple fact that we were all raised in varying family units makes every one of us different from another. By understanding our differences and our similarities, we add to the richness of life's journey. This happens when we are willing to open our minds to accept that others see the world differently than we see it.

Unravelling our beliefs and understanding the origin of these beliefs is key to discovering who we really are, and that can be very different from the person we were told to be. Self-discovery and self-reflection are necessary on a journey that requires letting go of outdated beliefs that no longer serve. This journey involves courage, acceptance, and forgiveness. Once I accepted things within myself and started celebrating what makes me happy, significant people in my life began to accept these things too. When we choose to grow, we bring people along with us on the journey. Over time, when everyone is open to perspectives different from their own, everyone wins. Understanding what makes you dance is a process.

Life Shines a Light on the Obvious

Before my affair, I believed I was a loyal person, but then I found myself in a situation beyond my comprehension. Eventually I was able to forgive myself when I started understanding what had lead Stu and me to that place. I discovered I am a passionate person who needs to be passionately loved. I discovered I married *The Provider* because, I had been told, my role was to raise children and to be the one who was provided for. My dad had said this in one way or another repeatedly, and my mom aligned with my dad's beliefs.

My affair and the adversity that went along with it opened my eyes to many perspectives. A younger, single man loved me in a way I hadn't been loved before. For the first time, I experienced passion and fun, and I wanted more. My affair gave me a glimpse into what it was like to be loved for who I was, not someone I was supposed to be.

In this process, I let go of my parents' perspectives along with who I believed they wanted me to be. By accepting who I was and forgiving myself for all the pain I caused, I was on the road that ultimately led me to finding Beau, the love of my life.

Gabe is a wise, nonjudgmental, and influential person in my life. Gabe was a minister at my church. I often felt like he was speaking to me directly, even though he was speaking to the entire congregation. His words were absorbed into my soul. One Sunday, Gabe said something like, "Love is being with someone who knows you and loves you anyway." Beau knows me and loves me anyway, and for that I'm very grateful. I'm not always easy to love.

You know that expression: *Once a cheater, always a cheater*. As you might imagine, it isn't my favourite expression. Obviously, I could cheat, there is no disputing that. With that awareness, Beau and I are aware of how important it is to celebrate our relationship. Relationships are delicate and life is difficult—a dangerous combination. Life presents many situations that can break the strongest relationships. When something is bothering Beau and me, we say it. We don't bottle things up within us, allowing issues to fester. It is the heartfelt conversations, and lots of them, that keep us connected. We spend hours talking with one another while we are walking, having a coffee, or drinking wine. We refer to these conversations as *foreplay*—need I say more?

Beau makes me dance. We enjoy working together and we continue to grow together. We are making a difference in our family, in business, and in people's lives. I am thankful for all the experiences that have led me to this place. Every decision, every choice we make, contributes to the fabric of our life.

I made choices that went against my own values and caused adversity in my life and in the lives of others. I made the choice to leave my marriage so I would be an example to my children as someone who chose life. There are consequences for every decision we make. I risked it all, followed my heart, and my heart led me to a passionate, fun-loving relationship that gives me joy and makes me dance.

Keeping life the same seems like the simplest solution, and in the short run, it can be. People generally resist change because change is uncomfortable. Change requires us to venture into the unknown and risk failure or risk being judged by others. Although change takes courage, change doesn't have to be this big monster that scares us. It can occur one small step at a time.

Your Turn: Adversity and Change

If you are feeling stuck in this moment, that's okay. Be kind to yourself. Most people have experienced feelings of helplessness after adversity has struck and left them in its wake. Adversity doesn't have to keep you stuck forever. After the initial blow, how we deal with adversity is fluid because the aftermath of adversity hits in waves. Think of the movement of the ocean tides. *Ebb* describes the tide receding back out to the sea, while *flow* describes the tide coming toward the land. The word *flow* can be used in such a different context than the flow mentioned in the previous chapter. Flow, in relation to adversity, means fluid. Adversity comes and it goes; it ebbs and it flows and leaves us forever changed.

Describe one thing in your life that you would like to change. It can be something small, like decluttering a closet, or it can be something bigger. Write down the first thing that comes to your mind.

I want to change: _____.

What is the first step to making this change? Let's say, for example, you want to have a healthier lifestyle. The first step could be to eat smaller portions. Still eat the same things, just a little less. Ultimately this one little choice will contribute to your goal.

My first step to making this change is: _____.

I will: _____.

Once eating smaller portions is manageable, add another change. Perhaps you want to eat more vegetables. You make the decision to have a salad for dinner instead of potatoes. This is another small change that, over time, makes a difference and keeps you moving toward your original goal of living a healthier lifestyle.

Change is scary if you look at it as something you need to do all at once. Change can be tackled in small, bite-sized pieces. Over time, these bite-sized pieces accumulate and make a big difference.

In your journal, describe how you imagine you will feel when you make this change in your life. How does this change align with your core values?

Insights:
Circle words, thoughts or phrases that stand out or surprise you. List insights below.

1.
2.
3.

Reframe:
Put these insights into a sentence that will inspire you to want to make this change in your life, one small step at a time.

When I _____(name the change from above)_____
I will feel _____ .

Changing _____ *in my life aligns with my core value:* _____.

Making this change is important to me because _____
_____ .

The first step I will take today toward making this change is _____ .

Your Turn: Getting Outside Your Comfort Zone

The definition of change is *to make or become different; to alter, vary, modify.* We all develop habits over time. These habits become a part of our way of being in the world. Habits can include eating certain foods, watching the same TV show day after day, staying up late, and sleeping well into the morning. These are examples of habits that make us feel safe.

When we decide we want to change one of our habits, we move from feeling comfortable to uncomfortable. One thing that makes us feel safe and secure is being altered/varied/removed from our life. This can be scary; it's like losing a security blanket. Habits that served us at one time in our life may no longer serve us. Eating certain foods may be bad for our health as we age. Watching the same TV show over and over may be taking you away from time you could be doing something more aligned with your current goals.

Whatever the reason, change will cause you to get outside your comfort zone. Start small, be consistent, and be kind to yourself. Change doesn't happen overnight. New habits take time to become a part of our lifestyle. If one day you slip back into an old habit, start again the next day. Be gentle with yourself; change can feel like a marathon, not a sprint.

Draw a circle in the middle of a page in your journal. Brainstorm all the things in your life that bring you comfort and write them within the circle. These could be your home, your friends, your family, certain foods you eat, your car, or bingeing a TV series. The list will be different for everyone. This circle represents your comfort zone.

Outside your comfort zone, write down what you want more or less of in your life. Time to yourself, more education, ability to travel, and learning a new skill are examples.

Circle one item outside your comfort zone, and describe how you imagine your life will be once you have achieved this:

When I achieve _____ *, my life will*

_____.

Describe how you will feel if you don't achieve this:

If I don't achieve _____ *, I will feel*

_____.

What three steps you will take to achieve this one thing outside your comfort zone?

    1.

    2.

    3.

This exercise can be applied to all the things you listed outside your comfort zone. If you're feeling inspired, keep going!

Chapter Ten

Family Brings You Closer to Your Purpose

You are given your family for a reason. Our family environments teach us the lessons we need to learn to become who we are meant to be. My parents did the best they could, given the tools they were given by their parents. The cycle continues in a pattern from one generation to the next. By being conscious of the lessons we were given and conscious of where the voices in our heads originate, we can change our script. Change starts with awareness.

I have come to think of my mom as my greatest role model. Although I mentioned my mom aligned and fell in step willingly with my dad's antiquated views of *Woman*, she has grown and transformed beyond those earlier years. Now in her nineties, my mom continues to be an inspiration, and I can thank all the adversity she has endured throughout her life for that. My dad's sudden death at age fifty-eight left my mom, also fifty-eight, to reinvent herself.

From my perspective, my dad was my mom's greatest love. My mom worked hard to finance my dad through law school. When my brother came along, my mom dedicated her life to raising a family and supporting my dad in his career. This worked for them. My brothers and I were fortunate to live in a household with two parents who loved one another deeply.

When my dad suddenly died, I remember standing in the receiving line of mourners, looking in disbelief at the open coffin and thinking how thankful I was that my dad was lying there and not my mom. This wasn't because I loved my mom more, I loved my dad equally for different reasons. Although I had only seen my parents together and my dad always came across as the one who made the decisions, I knew my mom would be okay. In that instant, it was clear my mom was the pillar of strength for my dad. Had my mom gone first, I believe my dad would have been like a rudderless sailboat, struggling to find his way. I didn't have the confidence in my dad's ability to carry on and thrive that I had in my mom's ability.

My dad died when I was thirty-one. For our entire lives, my brothers and I were given the *wait until your father gets home* line; it's a classic. We would live in fear of our dad walking through the door. It wasn't until he was taken from us that I discovered my mom's power and toughness. The message I received that day was both surprising and comforting. My mom has always been strong; her strength was simply overshadowed by my dad's presence. Adversity has a way of providing clarity. The message I received that day helped me through overwhelming grief.

When adversity strikes, it can strike hard, and it can take a while before we can stand. A friend of mine described adversity as a tsunami when it first hits. It knocks us over, and we feel like we will die. As time goes by, adversity becomes more like a tidal wave that knocks us down, allowing us to get our footing and stand eventually. As more time passes, adversity becomes a large wave that washes over us and leaves us standing. With time, the pain of adversity dissipates little by little. The pain is always there, but sooner or later, we're able to keep moving forward without being knocked down.

Grief changed me forever. Grief took a piece out of me, leaving a hole that has never completely healed. I can stand, can keep moving forward, albeit a little more cautiously than before.

I can only imagine the pain my mom felt within hours of my dad being gone. At first my mom was stoic. My mom delivered a eulogy honouring my dad that was a tribute to their relationship, our family, their friends, and Dad's dedication to his legal profession. Although much of the day has gone from my memory, I know the church was full, standing room only, with people waiting outside to pay tribute to my dad. I took comfort in knowing his life had impacted others.

My brothers and I lived away from home—two of us, a long way away. A few days after the funeral, my mom told us in no uncertain words that it was time for us to end our visit. She needed to grieve on her own, without all the chaos. My mom faced the loss of our dad head on. Alone in a big house they had built together, she made the choice to take one day at a time.

The next year, my mom went back to school. After two years, she became a lay preacher in the United Church of Canada. Decades before, my mom had had a spiritual experience that changed her life and brought her closer to God. Only when my dad passed did she give herself permission to follow this part of her journey. Had my dad lived, my mom would have continued to dedicate her life to fulfilling my dad's dreams.

My mom decided to reinvent herself. Adversity changed the course of her life and gave her the opportunity to do something she found meaningful, something that gave my mom purpose beyond my dad and the family.

Mom went on to marry again. She married a great guy who loved her from the moment they met. Two years into their relationship, he asked her to marry him. It took my mom eight years to accept. They were married and lived happily together for ten years before adversity struck, and my mom was alone again.

Unlike my dad, who dedicated his life to work, my mom has devoted her life to service. She has always been involved in church and in community.

When my dad died, my mom transformed. I'm sure the journey was gut-wrenching at times. She made the choice to create a new normal and to keep living life to the fullest. My mom has had a positive impact and continues to be an inspiration to many people. The adversity of my dad's passing gave my mom the opportunity to live her life's purpose. Mom has helped and been a friend, role model, and support when adversity has struck the lives of others.

My mom has continued to grow and evolve throughout her life. At eighty-five, she decided to sell her condo located in Toronto and move to the west coast of Canada. This was a courageous move because she had lived her entire life in the East. She went from the known to the unknown, and she did it with gusto.

Being from stoic British stock, my mom has endured struggles I don't really know about. On the outside, my mom wears a brave and happy demeanour. On the inside, she draws on her faith to give her direction and strength.

My mom moved into a community of active seniors. It wasn't long before she was calling everyone by name and introducing me to her new friends.

My mom faces adversity head on and makes tough decisions in her time and on her terms. Even in her nineties, my mom continues to be a force of nature.

Modelling the Behaviours of Our Parents

Our parents unintentionally teach us how to be in the world. As children, we watch, learn, and ultimately do what our parents model. Some of these behaviours serve us in life, and some don't. Through self-awareness and being conscious of where these behaviours originate, we can let go of certain behaviours and embrace others.

My dad taught me resilience. My father's dad died when he was sixteen, and his mom died when he was nineteen. Being an only child, my dad was forced to maneuver through the world alone. He turned to his uncle for support, and his uncle tried to cheat my dad out of receiving what was rightfully his from his parents' estate. This adversity was a blessing in disguise.

My grandmother wanted my dad to study medicine. To make his mom happy, he started studying sciences in university. Even though science didn't interest my dad, he went down this road anyway. When his uncle tried to cheat him, my dad started reading law to fight for what was his. Adversity and my dad's resilience set him on the right course. My dad said he was thankful for his uncle because without him, my dad would not have become a lawyer.

My father was a workaholic, and his workaholism was motivated by fear. Because he lost his parents at such an early age, he was driven to provide for his family. My dad didn't want his family to deal with the financial uncertainty he had endured. Ironically, it was probably this intense work focus that contributed to my dad's passing much too early.

Dad used to say he was "on borrowed time." At age fifty-six, he had outlived both his parents. Once he reached that age, he mentioned borrowed time often. In a way, it became a self-fulfilling prophecy. He died a month and a half before his fifty-ninth birthday.

There was a lot of heartache and a lot of adversity in my dad's life. He always bounced back with a brave face. He had a tough exterior; he wasn't as tough on the inside. Thankfully my mom and my dad met at a young age and my mom gave my dad the foundation, the love, and the strength he needed.

In preparation for Dad's funeral, I was tasked with creating two lines that best represented who he was to me. I had just over a handful of one-on-one times with my dad throughout my life. I spent four days with him on a business trip when I was nine, and he and I had five or so dinners by ourselves. It sounds crazy, but coming up with two lines was difficult. I value the one-on-one conversations we had; I wish we had shared more.

I have accepted that, like my dad, I have a tendency toward workaholism. Unlike my dad, I make time for my children and make sure I have lots of one-on-one time with each.

My dad taught me the most by modelling behaviours I didn't want to repeat as a parent, and for that I'm thankful. Unlike my dad, I keep my promises and try not to let work take priority. Instead of saying *family is important* and acting in ways that give the opposite message, I make time for my family. Instead of keeping things bottled up inside, I speak openly with people I love, and I am willing to have difficult conversations. I'm thankful my dad's behaviour provided a barometer for gauging who I am as a parent. I love my dad and am thankful for all the lessons he taught me, lessons I learned mostly through hurt feelings and observation.

The last time I spoke with him, he said, as he always did, "We love you."

I remember saying, "No, Dad—do *you* love me?" In that moment my dad told me "he" loved me. I told my dad I loved him twice in that phone conversation. Knowing this was our last conversation has helped me work through my grief.

Like our loyal pets who watch our every move, children watch us too. As children, we mimic our parents, and subconsciously, we become them. Through self-discovery and awareness, we can also consciously change these behaviours when we choose. In one of my favourite scenes from the sitcom *Friends*, Rachel is on a sailboat, barking out orders to people. She appears to have a realization. We see an actual *aha* moment. Rachel says, and I'm paraphrasing, "I've been so worried I was going to become my mother, and now I realize, I'm my father." She says, "I didn't see that coming!"

None of us see it coming. It's only when we raise our own children that our parents' behaviours really come to light. Parenting doesn't come with a manual, and if that's not daunting enough, when we co-parent with someone, a whole new medley of parenting is born. People bring their individual parenting styles, and sometimes this can cause conflict. Our parenting styles are as different as we are.

Understanding Where You've Been

A popular quote is: *You can't really know where you're going until you know where you have been.*

Some people are blessed with loving, caring parents, and some people cope with the opposite. We learn a lot of our parenting skills by how we have been raised. Our parents are only one example; there are lots of other parenting examples all around us, from neighbours, friends, and strangers. Although we all operate with our own parenting style, we can also learn as we go. Unravelling how you have been raised is a good beginning to understand who you are as a parent. Walk into any bookstore, and you'll find shelves of books filled with parenting advice. The trick is to sift and sort what works for you. Parenting is fluid, and your approach to parenting can evolve. Our kids were sent here to smooth off the rough edges. As parents, we teach our kids and when we're open, our kids teach us too.

When you answer the questions below, try to be open and not judge your answers. Freely list your answers in your journal. Part of a parent's job is to make mistakes. Our mistakes make us not only better parents, but better mentors for other parents. We are all works in progress, and we all have the choice to pass down or stop behaviours from our past.

Your Turn: Parenting

Who are you as a parent? Use the table below to help unravel your parenting behaviours, both where you've been and where you'd like to go:

	Behaviours I learned from my parents:	Behaviours from my parents I've rejected:	Behaviours that are my own:	Behaviours I want to model for my children:
1				
2				
3				
4				
5				

The list of behaviours you'd like to pass down to your children represents behaviours you feel are essential to who you are as a parent.

Insights:

Circle, highlight or underline behaviours that stand out.

1.
2.
3.

Reframe

How do you want to be remembered as a parent? Picture your children answering these questions about your parenting behaviour. Write a sentence, integrating your insights representing who you are as a parent at your best. This sentence describes behaviours you want to model for your children. Please write your sentence in the present tense starting with *I am*.

As a parent, I am: _____.

Chapter Eleven

Growth and Change ~ The Evolution of Motherhood

Who we are when we begin the journey of motherhood and who we are when our kids are adults is a progression. The only noise I hear as I sit in this quiet house is the sound of a clock ticking. In past years, this same house would have been alive with activity. During the chaos, I couldn't imagine that one day the commotion would come to an end. The days go by slowly and the years speed by, and then in a blink, the kids are gone and silence sets in.

I have been on journeys with my daughters that required me to evolve. Raising my daughters and being with them in adversity, I was shaped into a different person than I was when I started. My children and their journeys have impacted me immensely.

Most of us embark on our journey of motherhood naively, not knowing it is a transformational experience, full of complexities and emotional ups and downs. The journey starts from the moment of our child's conception.

My life was different from that moment on; maybe that's the way God planned it. I was more aware of my surroundings, what I was putting into my body, and my activities. My first pregnancy while I was with Stu resulted in miscarriage. Having a miscarriage was difficult for me on many levels. I was almost nine weeks pregnant when I started bleeding. The physical and emotional pain was excruciating. I remember arriving at the hospital in disbelief, unwilling to accept my reality. The male doctor told me to "be happy; at least you can conceive a child; many women cannot."

Happy, really?! It's hard for men to understand how difficult it is for women to go through this experience. Like the label on a bottle, men are on the outside of the birthing process looking in.

A well-meaning nurse gave me a magazine after the D&C procedure to take my mind off what had just happened. The cover featured a picture of a baby and a mother. I had dreamed of being a mother my whole life, and this dream had just been taken from me. I was beginning to grasp the magnitude of this loss. In these early moments of grief, I was hyper-aware of my surroundings with emotions close to the surface. When I expressed my sadness, this nurse understood. Ironically, she was overseeing a study to improve the patient's experience and met with me a few weeks later, when she told me she learned a valuable lesson that day. It's not easy to put ourselves into the shoes of others in these life-changing moments.

My dream of having a family was shattered, and although I found comfort in knowing I could conceive a child, I didn't know if I would be able to carry a child to term. I was devastated and felt the life I had envisioned was unattainable.

This experience highlighted how different Stu and I were with emotions. He coped by ignoring the pain and *getting on with it*. He believed miscarriage was a part of life. Stu didn't understand how traumatizing the experience was for me. He was incapable of understanding. I kept my feelings to myself and suffered in silence. As far as Stu was concerned, the miscarriage was behind us, and it was time to move on. This event marked the beginning of the end for Stu and me.

Adversity brings out who we really are. It shines a light and illuminates the core of who we are. I couldn't see this at the time. That experience created the first crack in our marriage. As years passed, when the crack became wider, I would fill it with the chaos of more children. Family chaos was the plaster I used to fill the gap. Eventually the crack grew so wide, it was beyond repair and separated us.

The Joys and Challenges of Motherhood

About eight months after the miscarriage, we were pregnant again. Reese arrived in the world. Reese was a miracle of life. I stayed in the hospital for a week. Having the comfort of nurses who knew what they were doing was a relief. The ride home from the hospital was scary because the time had come for us to step up and start making parenting decisions without nurses, without a manual, without a clue.

Being a mother for the first time is a surreal experience. I had been working in a career, and the next day, I had this little human with me every minute, dependent on me for survival. My parents lived across the country. I felt alone most of the time. At times it was joyous, sometimes terrifying, frustrating, challenging, and often a thankless experience. Motherhood took me through a whole spectrum of emotions.

I enjoyed being a mom. Reese and I spent lots of time outside walking and being in the fresh air. She was a perfect, easygoing, happy child during the day. Every evening, like clockwork, just as Stu arrived home from work, Reese would start screaming at the top of her lungs for hours. It was an uncontrollable, inconsolable cry. Stu and I endured this nightmare for six months until what we believed was evening colic finally ran its course. I wondered what I had done wrong and how I could be such a terrible mom. Thankfully I had wonderful days with Reese that made up for the blood-curdling screams that Stu and I endured together in the evening hours.

After giving my all to my daughter during the day, I had little time or energy to give to Stu. For six months, it was impossible to speak through the anguished screams.

I laugh when people say a child brings a couple closer; that's one of life's greatest lies.

Between 1988 and 1996, I had four daughters. After Reese came Kendra, then Eve, and at last, Mila.

When my children were seven and under, I called five o'clock the "witching hour." At the end of most days, my kids were tired, grumpy, and hungry. To meet the demands of all four kids and still get dinner on the table, I made dinner while breastfeeding Mila, holding her like a football so I could do it all. Being a dog lover, I brought a puppy into the mix when I was pregnant with Kendra.

Motherhood has been a balancing act and a journey of funny, humbling, and life-changing experiences. Stu was focused on growing his career, and following my mom's example, I looked after the family and everything related to our home. I felt fortunate to be a stay-at-home mom and believed it was a privilege that came with unexpected challenges.

When we were living in my hometown of London, Ontario, while out doing many errands, the engine of my van stopped. There was enough forward momentum to get the van safely off the road into what just happened to be the driveway of the office where my dad had worked. He had been gone for many years, but his name was still on the sign. When I walked into the reception area to call a tow truck, the first thing I saw was my dad's picture on the wall. I thanked him for watching over me and for guiding my van to safety. I remember thinking how happy he would be, knowing my van wasn't blocking access for clients to come and go.

The van was towed, and I was assured it was fixed and safe to drive the next day. The girls and I were driving to meet their dad in Toronto for a weekend adventure. Mila was just a couple of months old; Eve was three, Kendra five, and Reese seven. I was breastfeeding Mila at the time and had a vision of pulling over to feed her en route. The journey between London and Toronto is about two hours along a busy highway. Everything was going smoothly until we were driving into Toronto. I could see Lake Ontario in the distance and was internally breathing a sigh of relief, until I saw steam coming out from under the hood of the van. I had to remain calm on the outside for the girls' sake. On the inside, I was freaking out. I found my way to a parking lot situated behind a waterfront hotel. I didn't know what to do. Stu was thirty-eight thousand feet in the air and would be arriving from Vancouver.

I parked and got the kids out of the car, carrying Mila in her car seat. I wandered toward the hotel lobby and spotted a stranger. I told this kind stranger about our predicament and how we desperately needed to find a gas station. This good samaritan dropped what he was doing, jumped back into his car, and said, "Follow me."

That's exactly what I did, I followed him in my van for a few blocks, through busy back roads. He stuck his arm out of his car, pointed to a gas station and kept going.

Just as I turned into the gas station, the heat gauge swung immediately past the highest temperature. We had seconds to spare. When the van was supposedly fixed in London, they had used an old part that was cracked. On the drive to Toronto, the engine overheated, and the broken piece had punctured the radiator, draining the van of water.

Being a mom requires us to think on our feet and stay calm in times of crisis. As a mom, I never knew what was around the corner, but I had confidence I would deal with whatever came my way with unrelenting courage and super-human problem-solving skills. I didn't realize the transformational power moments like these had on me. I was evolving without knowing it.

Silent, Transformational Change

This evolution took place every day, silently, relentlessly, and consistently. The simple act of grocery shopping turned into an adventure. All five of us would jump into what my kids later referred to as the *loser cruiser* and venture to an enormous superstore where prices were reasonable. Inevitably two kids would fight to ride in the cart and eventually there would be three following along. I would load food on top of the daughter who had won the turn to ride, eventually the mound of groceries squeezing her out of the cart to be with the rest of her sisters. While we were shopping, the girls could choose one thing we would all share while shopping and pay for at the end, usually a box of cookies or bag of Jujubes.

I was constantly counting heads, ensuring all my kids were in tow. One time, to my horror, I only counted three. I immediately got that sick feeling in the pit of my stomach. Mila, four years old at the time, was gone. I asked the girls if they had seen her, and they just casually shook their heads. I went into panic mode, ran to customer service with my three girls, and let customer service know my daughter was missing. Over the loudspeaker, I heard them announce *a child is missing* and felt the horror—that missing child was mine! After many agonizing minutes, Mila was found, and the crisis was over. Decades later, I can still remember the feeling of both terror and relief. This was an instance in motherhood when minutes seemed to last a lifetime.

I did the best I could to mother with the tools I was given, and once I exhausted these tools, I survived on instinct. I would hear my kids mimic what I had said and was reminded they were watching and absorbing every behaviour I modelled, consciously or unconsciously. These little humans were developing their beliefs based on my beliefs. Being a parent comes with enormous responsibility.

Children need to define themselves within the family unit. They need to find something that is extraordinary and makes them stand out. Reese was the rebel who demanded attention. When she decided anorexia would no longer define her, basketball became her thing. Kendra was the academic and the master of the funny one-liner. Eve was the fashion model and the thoughtful observer. Mila had to find something that was notably hers, too, when everything seemed to be taken.

Beau is the one who helped Mila find her way. When he came into our lives, he saved us. We saved Beau too. Paying the bills, keeping a roof over our heads, and being a lone parent had been overwhelming.

Surviving the Teenage Years

I was relieved when we made it through the difficult teenage years. When my daughters screamed *I hate you!* at the top of their lungs, I stopped hearing those words because I had heard them so many times. I would suggest they be a little more original next time by telling me something I hadn't heard hundreds of times before. *I hate you!* was often accompanied with the slamming of a door. When they were newly licensed to drive, it was scary when *I hate you!* was shouted right before they got behind the wheel and put the *pedal to the metal* to go tell their dad what a terrible person I was.

Being raised in two very different households, it was easy for my girls to play one parent against the other. They were skilled; they knew the right buttons to push and the right things to say to get one parent on their side. I often had to step back to realize how I was being drawn into their manipulative game.

Stu was okay with hearing disrespectful things said about me; he seemed to like it. His girls were confirming what I suspected were his inner thoughts. The girls always had a place to go when tempers were high under my roof. They always had a retreat.

I'm thankful all four didn't act out at once. It was usually one at a time. One day, the behaviour in our household was so over-the-top, I decided to call a family meeting. This was still early days with Beau, so family meant Stu, the girls, and me. These meetings were the dreaded *living room meetings* where there was no playing one parent against the other. In these meetings, Stu and I presented a united front.

On this occasion, Reese was defiant, and Kendra followed her example. As we gathered in the living room, Kendra had a blanket over her head. Eve and Mila were watching and learning. At one point, Reese stormed out of the house, refusing to participate. This was a moment of truth—it was time for me to draw a line in the sand and send the message that enough is enough. To save the other three, the time had come for me to send Reese to live with her dad. It was unacceptable to speak to someone the way Reese spoke to me, and I needed to deliver this message for Reese's ultimate happiness and well-being. It was time my other three girls saw me take a stand.

When Beau returned from a peaceful walk with Rox and was curious how the meeting went, I responded, "It was the worst ever." The next day, I asked Reese to leave the house to live with her dad permanently. That decision was one of the hardest and the best decisions I made as a mom. Reese and I have a mutually respectful and loving relationship today.

Lessons From My Girls

I have learned to forgive myself for not being the perfect mother. In forgiving myself, I have been able to forgive my parents too. Our mistakes help our children in the long run; they are part of the children's journey. I am thankful my girls as adults choose to spend time with me, despite the mistakes I have made. They love me anyway. The words of my wise minister-friend, Gabe, apply to relationships with children too: "Love is someone who knows you and loves you anyway." Despite all the mistakes we make as parents, when our children know us and love us anyway, it's a blessing—one I am grateful for every day.

Just as my parents did the best they could, I have done the best I can raising my daughters. I often joke about the therapy my kids will need when they are older and how most of the conversation will revolve around me. Part of our job as parents is giving our kids circumstances to work through as they mature. Sifting and sorting experiences we've had, differentiating between our truth and someone else's—these are necessary steps on the journey toward understanding what makes each of us dance in our own way.

As much as I tried to impart my wisdom to my girls, they taught me a lot too. I needed to learn to let go of control. I couldn't protect my daughters from feeling pain; I could only support them through it. I learned my journey is not their journey. My lessons are different from the lessons my daughters will learn in their lifetime. Their lessons are related to discovering their life purposes, and their purposes are different from mine.

Motherhood taught me humility. Motherhood has taught me to laugh at myself. Sometimes if I didn't laugh, I would cry. I've learned laughing is more fun than crying.

Motherhood has taught me to be kind to myself and to forgive myself for the mistakes I've made. I understand unconditional love. Nothing stops me from loving my kids unconditionally. To experience joy, we must also experience sorrow, and being a mother brings both emotions in unexpected and unimaginable ways.

I learned to pick my battles. Some arguments are not worth having. Many arguments don't matter and will be forgotten. As long as no one was hurt, I learned I had to let my kids discover their own solutions, a skill they will use throughout their life. Not all battles are mine to fight. My daughters must learn to fight their own battles. It's a rite of passage.

Through all the difficulties, the screw-ups, the *I hate you*s, the door-slamming, tough love, and marriage breakup, my daughters are making their way in the world. Reese has her daughter Kenzie, and I get to witness Reese's journey through motherhood. As a grandmother, I am no longer on the frontline. I can observe without being the disciplinarian. It's a different vantage point, one I struggle with at times. My desire to control lies just beneath the surface and peeks through often.

Motherhood is a privilege. When my daughters were young, I couldn't see an end to all the chaos and confusion. Knowing what I know now, time goes by in a blink. My dad used to say, "Don't wish your life away." I get it now. Our children grow within us and become a part of us at the moment of conception. Perhaps this is the reason we mothers assume so much guilt when our children's lives go off track.

It's the little things that matter: the traditions and the memories. Together they make up the fabric of a family, something my kids will be trying to unravel long after I'm gone. I learned to keep the lines of communication open, especially when I wasn't going to like what I was about to hear. I learned to trust the process and not to hold on too tight. Letting my kids fall and get back up on their own has given them the strength they needed to maneuver their way through life. When I became a mom, I thought it was my role to teach my children, and I discovered it was a two-way street. My daughters were sent here to teach me too.

Raising children has a way of smoothing rough edges. Raising kids has kept me on the edge of my seat wondering what would happen next. What a ride!

Motherhood ~ The Evolution of You

Although no two experiences of motherhood are exactly the same, there are similarities. As our children grow, so do we. Our children take us along for the ride of our lives as we help them become the people they are meant to be. It's natural to feel lost in this journey. It's one that's all consuming and full of risks and obstacles.

Becoming lost in the journey is sometimes our only means of survival. Parenting can take most of what we have to give. Once we have provided our kids their roots, including their values, their street smarts, their coping mechanisms, their sense of self, it's time to restore ours and emerge as a different person from where we began. This starts with understanding who we were when we started and who we are now as our kids grow into adults. Evolution happens at every stage of the journey, without us even knowing. Change happens silently and mysteriously behind the chaos.

We learn a lot from our parents, and often what we've learned is so deeply imbedded in who we are and how we behave, it is difficult to separate the two. As moms, we try to figure it out on the job. This is complex.

Your Turn: Mothering

In your journal, contemplate these guiding thoughts and questions:

Who were you when you first became a mom?

Name an adversity you endured along the journey:

*I endured:*_____.

What was the silver lining you discovered on the other side of adversity?

How have you evolved because of this adversity?

Insights:

List thoughts and phrases that stand out for you in your answers.

1.
2.
3.

Reframe:

Integrate these thoughts and phrases into a sentence that represents how you have grown as a person through the journey of motherhood:

I have: _____.

What do you want to do with this more-evolved you?

Please complete this sentence:

I will make a difference in the world by: _____.

Chapter Twelve

Finding What Makes You
Dance in Love

Relationships build upon one another, one piece at a time. Every relationship leads us to where we are today. In love, you are here because of decisions you have made.

Because I had given so much of myself to my children physically, emotionally, and mentally, I reached the point where I wondered: *Is this all there is? What about me?* and *Where do I fit beyond being a mother?* The journey to figure out what made me dance was accompanied with heartache, tears, and soul-searching. I had to let go and trust the process. For someone like me, who prefers to control her life and everyone in it, that was challenging. Often through tears, I was forced to *let go and let God* take the reins, relying on my faith that everything would be okay.

My journey began by unravelling the fabric of my life. By identifying the things that worked and the things that no longer served me, I could better understand influences on my choices. The parts of my past that no longer served me had power over me until I was able to acknowledge them consciously and send them on their way. Although experiences and feelings reappear, they no longer own me.

When my marriage was in trouble, my mom gave me the "Serenity Prayer," adopted and popularized by Alcoholics Anonymous and other twelve-step programs:

> *God grant me the serenity to accept the things*
> *I cannot change, courage to change the things*
> *I can, and wisdom to know the difference.*

My mom wanted me to stay in the marriage, believing it was something I must accept and could not change. For me, I knew staying in my marriage would cause my soul to die, and I would be giving my children the message that being unhappy and unfulfilled in a lifeless relationship is okay.

My mom also told me she thought I should continue having affairs. Although that was the situation in which I found myself, I knew deep down being in an affair wasn't what I wanted. I wanted to be loyal. An affair is a symptom of a relationship that isn't working and a sign something needs to change. I wasn't willing to sacrifice my happiness—and, ultimately, my children's happiness—in a marriage that was broken.

My mom and I saw the same prayer from two different perspectives. My mom wanted me to accept my situation and be disloyal to endure it. Her perspective came from her desire to protect me and her grandchildren because the road ahead was unknown and scary. I saw this prayer and thought: *I've got this—I can change my situation*, and I needed a ton of courage to make changes and protect my children from watching Stu's and my relationship implode even further.

Ultimately, I found what makes me dance in love, in family, in career, and in faith. God gave me the courage to change the things I could and the wisdom to know the difference.

Relationship Decisions Based on the Stories We're Told

Every experience, heartbreak, relationship—even the ones with our parents, siblings, and friends—influences who we choose as our life partner. These influencers are in the background, swaying our decision in one way or another both consciously and subconsciously. I unravelled the impact significant people and experiences had in my life, so I could uncover what makes me dance in love.

I experienced my first true love in high school. Will was a kind and generous guy who holds a permanent place in my heart. Will was a football player, a shot putter, an overall great athlete. To my dad's dismay, he didn't aspire to go to university, and therefore, didn't align with my family's values. Will was a wonderful guy who made me feel safe. We had fun together; we laughed and experienced a lot of *firsts* together. In the movie, *How to*

Deal (2003, director: Clare Kilner), a wise grandmother tells her granddaughter, "You know dear, first loves are never really over." That is my experience. My first love will forever have a special place in my heart.

The way a relationship ends matters. My relationship with Will ended when I went to university because my dad wanted it to, and I complied. Because this relationship didn't end naturally, it took on a life of its own and stayed with me for decades. I argued with my dad about Will. He would say, "He is a great guy . . . for someone else's daughter." I was surrounded with many other *fish in the sea* who were on the same track as me, but no one compared to Will.

Relationships form a mosaic of experiences that provide wisdom and insight. Will had an impact on my heart, and it was difficult for me to let him go. The first guy I dated at university had little chance, especially when he refused to hold my hand. *That's the end of him!* I told myself. *Will would never have done that.* My dad told me if I didn't meet someone in university, I would never meet anyone, and I believed him. I went into my fourth year determined to find the person with whom I was going to spend the rest of my life.

One night after the reluctant hand-holder and I had gone our separate ways, I saw a guy I had never noticed before walk down the stairs from the bar where my girlfriends and I had been. We made eye contact, and this momentary glance was the beginning.

My girlfriends and I went to another bar, and this same guy (Stu) asked me to dance. I said yes, and that simple dance changed the course of both our lives. I was on a mission to meet someone to spend my life with. In my early twenties, I didn't question my dad's perspective—I acted on it. I was young, naive, and impressionable to accept my dad's truth as my own. That night, stars aligned, and my future was cast.

Team sport was a big part of my family's culture growing up. This is probably one of the reasons I felt comfortable with Will. Will's athletic ability and love for sport aligned with some of the good parts of my family. My breakup with Will was the beginning of a quiet rebellion within me. Stu hadn't played any team sports. I was attracted to Stu because of his academic ability. I rejected a part of my family's culture when I married Stu. I conformed to my dad's wishes by marrying someone with a university education and lost an important piece of my family, and me, in the process. This is one of life's paradoxes.

The ideology of team sport infiltrates almost every aspect of life. Team sport is the foundation for many of my core values. When I made the decision to marry Stu, I didn't realize I was marrying someone whose values were vastly different from mine.

My mom told me when I was a girl that it wasn't possible to find someone who was both driven and emotionally connected. That set me up perfectly to marry Stu, who was driven, university-educated, and emotionally disconnected. All boxes were ticked.

Interestingly, my dad also was driven to a fault and emotionally disconnected. My grandfather on my mom's side was also career driven with limited ability to connect emotionally. My mom was projecting her life experience onto me, and I accepted it as my own. Putting together the pieces, it took me having an affair and my dad's and E's passing to realize my life is not my mom's life, and my story is not my mom's story. Through self-discovery and adversity, I was able to free myself and create a life on my terms to keep moving forward.

When I decided I had had enough and could summon the courage to leave my marriage and leap into the unknown, I met Beau. Beau, the love of my life, is driven, emotionally connected, university-educated, and a former professional athlete.

Making choices that seem right, given the information we have at the time, is all we can do.

Your Turn: Unravelling the Messages From Relationships

Look back at your relationships and notice how they piece together. We all have voices in our heads that originate from other people. Even when these people have gone, their voices remain. It's possible to set free those voices that no longer serve you. Identify the origin of the voices. Keep the voices that serve you; acknowledge and let go of the voices that hold you back. Negative voices are powerful and will get in our way and stop us from discovering our true essence and what makes us dance, in all aspects of our lives.

Before any of us can make changes in our lives, we need first to unravel the stories we have been told. The key is understanding whether these stories help us move forward or stop us in our tracks. The first step is uncovering what those messages are.

In your journal, make a table like the one below. List messages you received in the impressionable years from significant people in your life in two columns: those that serve you and those you would like to let go or release.

	Messages I've received:	Messages that no longer serve me:
Message 1		
Message 2		
Message 3		

Insights:
List thoughts and phrases from the column that stand out.
1.
2.
3.

Reframe:
Now, put these messages in your own words. By rewriting these messages, you can move forward on your own terms, not on someone else's. Put these three insights into a sentence that frees you from messages that no longer serve you and stop you in your tracks.

Finish this sentence:
I am free to: _____.

Now that you have discovered this new sense of freedom, what are you going to do with it? Complete this sentence.
I will: _____ .

Chapter Thirteen

Relationships

In the movie *Pretty Woman* (1990, director: Garry Marshall), Edward climbs up the fire escape and asks Vivian "So what happens after he climbed up the tower and rescued her?"

She answers, "She rescues him right back."

Beau rescued me, and I rescued him right back.

Beau came into our family and brought a sense of calm and humour that was new. Although a marriage breakup isn't ideal, after the initial shock has dissipated, happy parents ultimately make for happy children.

When Beau entered the scene, Mila was nine and Reese was sixteen, with Eve and Kendra in between. I was outnumbered by hormonal teenagers who thought they had the answers, even though their brains weren't fully formed. Every month our periods would sync, and Beau would be surrounded by five menstruating females. Beau was the only male in the house—even our pets were female. When we first officially started dating, Beau had his own apartment. It became our escape on days the girls were with their dad. We felt like kids again. We were thankful for our time together because it gave us space to grow our relationship, away from teenage drama and chaos.

Trusting Intuition

My girls had endured my relationship with a man before Beau that left a scar. I refer to him as *Transition Guy*.

Six months after Transition Guy's and my relationship ended, our paths crossed at the gym. When I told him I was seeing someone else, something within him snapped. After finishing my workout, I went to the parking lot where my loyal pooch Rox was sleeping in the passenger seat. Transition Guy followed me to my car. Rox knew him, and she could sense something was wrong. There was a strange darkness in his eyes as he spoke. Rox kept looking at me and then at him, like she was assessing the situation and getting ready to protect me if necessary. Luckily Rox and I got out of the parking lot unscathed.

For months, I had refused to read any emails Transition Guy sent, and this was a great frustration for him. He had lost the control he once had. During our relationship, I'd try to break up with him, but he'd manipulate his way back. I let it happen; that's on me. A few days after our encounter at the gym, I received a flood of emails consisting of only subject lines with made-up domain names. The subject lines were all different, and they told a story—my story. Transition Guy became so obsessed with the idea that I had moved on, he had taken the time to segment every painful part of my life into domain names and subject lines, so I would have no alternative but to see them.

I was working with Beau at the time, and together, we decided the right thing to do was call the police. I went home, copied all the emails, called the police, and waited for twenty-four hours. Finally, an empathetic officer came to the house. After she read the emails, she said Transition Guy was escalating and needed to be stopped. She said when people in this state get a visit from the police, things can escalate further. She advised us to get out of the house for a couple of days and go somewhere safe he didn't know about.

Eve, Mila, two of their friends, Rox, and I went to Beau's place where we created a fun adventure, while Reese and Kendra went to their dad's. We were in a secure building in a different part of the city.

The following week, after receiving the first flood of emails, before the police paid Transition Guy a visit, I received several more. This time when I called the police, a male police officer arrived at my house within the half-hour. He kindly asked how I was doing and then promptly advised me to sever all ties with Transition Guy, and that meant severing ties with his children.

I couldn't bring myself to do that. I am still in contact with his children today. I weighed the pain of letting his kids go out of my life against the threat I believed he posed. My brothers were concerned for my safety and hired a private detective to follow Transition Guy.

The private eye assured me he was staying away and was heeding the police warning. I was fortunate. Every situation is different, and all factors need to be weighed carefully in potentially threatening situations.

It took therapy to let go of the terror and residual trauma resulting from this experience. At first, I would experience a fight-or-flight response when I saw him in the community. After receiving EMDR (Eye Method Desensitization and Reprocessing) therapy that targeted this experience, I was able to view him as an annoyance, not a threat.

Now I see him as a cowardly cyber-bully who tried to hurt and manipulate me. This relationship contributed to my strength, and it taught me to trust my instincts. I knew he was trouble long before I decided to end the relationship. Something allowed me to be manipulated. This relationship gave me insight into who I am and the wisdom to trust my instincts and my inner voice.

Beau supported me emotionally through this experience and made the girls and me feel safe. This situation accelerated the bond we all felt toward him. When he came into the family, he was a breath of fresh air. I could hear a collective sigh of relief from my girls that Transition Guy was out of our life for good.

Every romantic relationship we have brings a wealth of information about what works and what doesn't and is an opportunity to learn more about ourselves. By consciously thinking about what fits and what doesn't, I was able to trust my instincts in my relationship with Beau.

First Loves Are Never Really Over

Early on in my relationship with Beau, I needed to know if I could finally move on emotionally from my first love, Will. My dad did his best to steer me away from Will, but my heart had a different plan, I had loved Will for thirty years. Beau and I were visiting Nova in my hometown. With Beau's blessing, I had breakfast with Will.

Getting ready to meet Will was a very strange experience, one I could hardly believe I was having. I was like this giddy teenager, and Beau calmly and confidently encouraged me.

During breakfast with Will, I discovered how much I had grown and changed. Through raising a family, having a career, and surviving a marriage breakup, I was different. I enjoyed our time together and our breakfast provided closure. I came away from my reunion with Will appreciating Beau's deep love and support for me.

It comes down to knowing how you feel when you are with a person. Attracting the right person includes knowing who you are and what you are looking for in a relationship. Relationship experiences from the past can play out in current relationships. Past relationships hold the most power when we aren't aware this power exists. Minimizing the impact of past relationships begins with understanding why these relationships packed such a punch in the first place. Let's begin to unravel the reasons behind why certain relationships stay with you. This way you can better understand what you want and what you won't accept in future relationships.

Aligned Values ~ The Foundation for Lasting Relationships

My relationship with Beau works, and I attribute this to our aligned values. We share the same values in business, family, money, love, and faith. Our aligned values allow us to avoid power struggles. Our need to win, to be seen, and to be heard is in alignment, and generally we want the same things out of life, and we move in the same direction.

Because Beau and I had worked closely together, I was able to learn a lot about him. Before romance became a part of who we were together, I knew Beau was a great father who had a respectful relationship with the mother of his children. It was important for me that Beau had friends, a sense of humour, and a strong work ethic.

Coming from the *macho* hockey world, I was concerned Beau was homophobic and this misalignment of values would end our relationship. I was with my cousin Sam, crying as I shared my fear about Beau. Sam owned two bars, and one was a gay bar, notorious for wild parties. Sam set the wheels in motion to discover if Beau was homophobic.

For someone new to the scene, Sam's bar was memorable. Beau was looking forward to the experience and had no idea he was being tested. We walked up this long staircase and were greeted by the host—a tall, outgoing, and very welcoming drag queen. We turned the corner to see the men serving drinks were all wearing loin cloths. The theme of the night was "Gone Wild," and mid-afternoon, it seemed the evening was heading that way. This was pure entertainment. I knew a lot of Sam's friends, so I fit right in. This was new, uncharted territory for Beau.

Beau experienced what it was like to stand in line for the washroom. As women, we know that line too well. Patiently, Beau waited his turn. Just as he reached the urinals, a gentleman lamented loudly that all the good-looking guys were gone, and then he looked right at Beau and said, for all to hear, "Not *all* the good-looking guys are gone!" Beau finally appeared back at our table, looking pale. He told me the story and I roared with laughter. Sam and I couldn't have orchestrated anything better.

Soon after the washroom encounter, I saw Beau speaking intently to Brad, the person Beau had met by the urinals. Not surprisingly, Brad had found Beau in the crowd and the two were engrossed in conversation. Beau played in the NHL and has an extensive hockey background through coaching his children in the sport. Brad also came from a family where hockey was an integral part of the family culture. His parents billeted young hockey players in their home. Beau and Brad were discussing what it was like for Brad to be gay and raised by homophobic parents. Brad shared how his parents found him during an intimate act with a young billet.

Beau was surprised and saddened to hear that Brad's parents blamed Brad and kicked him out of the house at a very young age. Through Brad's story, Beau gained insight into the cruelty, the anguish, and the pain caused by homophobia.

Brad was put in Beau's path for a reason. Beau later shared how, in the male-dominated hockey culture, he had regrettably said thoughtless things to fit in. I was relieved to learn that Brad's treatment by his family went profoundly against Beau's values.

Brad was an icon in the gay community and was a leader in the gay rights and gay activism in Vancouver. He encouraged people to love one another for both their similarities and their differences. The encounter between Brad and Beau shone a light on Beau's values and was divinely meant to be. After a *wild night* with loin cloths, long bathroom lines, revealing conversations, and discreet observations, Beau passed the test.

Watch any romantic comedy, read any love story, and it seems we are all looking for the same thing: our one true love. Most of us go through life searching for true love and settle for someone. It's a miracle when the stars align, people cross paths, and circumstances allow two soulmates to be together.

Beau and I often talk about what it would have been like if we had met earlier. We both agree we met exactly when we were supposed to. Both of us had to go through a lot of adversity and endure a lot of heartache before we were ready to meet.

We now understand we were simultaneously enduring challenges that ultimately bonded us together. Only God knew. We were a part of a bigger plan. On that fateful walk with my dog Rox, when that voice within asked: *What makes you dance?* I had no idea I would meet someone who makes me dance. Not only did Beau save me, but he also brought fun, laughter, and lighthearted banter into our house. He saved my girls too.

Family Tradition and the Reflection of Values

The same values that bond Beau and me together bond our children and grandchildren together as well. When my first marriage ended and Stu and I were living in different households, I created traditions to foster certain values within my children that continue today. We kick off Christmas with a *Make a Gift* tradition. We draw one name and make something—a gift that comes from thought, creativity, and love. My girls loved to hate this tradition.

We still laugh about Kendra, wrapping a candy cane in a twenty-dollar bill in protest. Over the years, the Make a Gift has become more elaborate, and I'm amazed by the creations. It's my favourite Christmas tradition. Taking time, putting thought into a gift, and presenting it with love is a significant part of Christmas magic.

When Beau joined this family tradition, he brought a male energy and a kid-like uneasiness that was fun to witness. Beau will angst about his Make a Gift as much as we do. I receive great joy from seeing Beau stringing beads at our local bead shop or painting pottery at a ceramics studio. At first, Beau would say, "if my hockey buddies could see me now. ..." Our Make a Gift tradition has become a rite of passage into our family. Boyfriends and partners are now tasked with this tradition when they join our family.

One year, I was overwhelmed with all the things that needed to get done and suggested to the girls that perhaps we skip Make a Gift that year. Much to my surprise, I almost had a revolt on my hands. Under no circumstances were my girls letting me take the tradition away. It has been woven into our family experience, and it grounds us. This tradition is a symbol of our family values, and it contributes to making our family who we are. It took a while to take root; now it's part of us and has the power to live on long after I'm gone.

One Christmas when the girls were all home from living away or at university, Beau, the girls, and I got family tattoos. I never thought I would string those words together. This tattoo symbolizes how our blended family had taken hold in all our hearts.

The tattoo place was at street level in Gastown, an edgy part of Vancouver. People walking by the studio would look in and stare. It must have been quite a sight with all six of us getting inked. My girls are all close to or over six feet tall. They turn heads when they walk down the street. Eventually the owners had to put opaque screens in the windows to discourage onlookers.

Each tattoo is a puzzle piece that bears a different letter from the word ALWAYS. We are individuals who fit together. Beau is a part of our family, and we each have a tattoo to celebrate and commemorate the love we have for one another.

Families are complex. Blended families, even more so. Our families, with my four daughters and Beau's two sons and daughter have blended smoothly. His kids were adults when we met, and they wanted their dad to be happy. Although my daughters were still living at home, Beau's kids were adults with their own places, so we weren't all living under the same roof. This made the process of blending much easier.

The complexities of family become more apparent when kids choose their life partner. The married-ins bring their own set of values.

I have discovered boyfriends, sons, and sons-in-law diffuse the emotional tension that exists between women. Although this is a broad generalization, boys fight physically; girls fight with words. A look from one of my daughters packs a punch. Women communicate differently from men. I know where I stand in every interaction with my daughters and daughters-in-law. I weathered many emotional storms while raising my girls, and this prepared me to have a blended family of strong-willed women who share their opinions openly and without hesitation.

I am playing my part to encourage all our children and our grandchildren to be the best they can be and to strive to find their purpose. Families and communities are happier and healthier when people live their life purpose and find what makes them dance.

While shared values make our family work, it is love that fuels our values. Love has evolved and grown between our kids. I observe our daughters and daughters-in-law bonding over conversations about their children, their careers, and other life obstacles. Together, we have become stronger.

Every situation is different, and with blending families, there is no *one size fits all*. It's taken drama, patience, laughter, and tears to get to this place, and we protect our blended family unit. It is ours, and it works, even with all its complexities and moving parts. We don't take this relationship for granted. Open, heartfelt communication and love keeps our blended family unit strong.

Your Turn: Relationships

Think about the romantic relationships you have had in your life. List two to three relationships you consider to be significant. The length of time doesn't matter as much as the impact this person has had on you. In your journal, answer the questions below about these relationships.

Name: _____.
What do you like about this person? _____.
What don't you like about this person? _____.
What would you change in this person? _____.
How do you feel when you're with this person?
_____.

What does this relationship teach you about yourself?

_____.

Knowing what you know after being in this relationship, what are you *willing to accept* in future relationships?

_____.

Knowing what you know after being in this relationship what are you *not willing to accept* in future relationships?

_____.

Insights:
Highlight, underline, or circle words or phrases that stand out. Look for consistencies across these relationships. List them below.

1.
2.
3.

Reframe:
Please finish this sentence.
I am happiest in a relationship when: _____.

Your Turn: Aligning Values

Every decision you make reflects your values and your beliefs. Your values are core to who you are. Values are your guiding compass. They shape how you move through the world. Your values influence your relationships, your family, personal development, and your career path. When values are out of alignment, they can also influence your emotional, mental, and physical health.

In this exercise, think of two people in your life: one with whom the relationship is easy and one with whom it is difficult. Write the names in the first column.

In the next column, list your most important core values from the previous exercise.

Next, put a ✓ or an x beside your value, indicating whether this person shares your same core value.

Write what you know or have learned about yourself. It can be as simple as: *I must have fun in my life, and fun does not seem important to this person.*

The point of this exercise is to shine a light on why some relationships seem easier than others. It is usually a direct reflection of core values alignment or misalignment.

	My Core Values	✓ or x	What I Know About Myself:
Person One:			
Person Two:			

Insights:
Circle, highlight, or underline thoughts or phrases that stand out. List three insights you have learned about yourself.

1.
2.
3.

Reframe:
Think about how you feel when you're with someone whose values are out of alignment with yours. In contrast, now think about how differently you feel when you're with someone whose values align. Please describe below.

Finish these sentences:
When my values are out of alignment with the person I'm with, I: _____
_____.

When my values are in alignment with the person I'm with, I: _____
_____.

Chapter Fourteen

Bringing It All Together

We are evolving and being shaped with each passing day. Past experiences can stop us or inspire us to change. New experiences and encounters prepare us for what's ahead.

Your Three-Circle Model

On a large piece of paper, draw three intersecting circles, using a different colour for each circle. Label one circle HIGH SCHOOL, one ROLES, and the last, VALUES. In the middle of the intersection circles, write your name or ME.

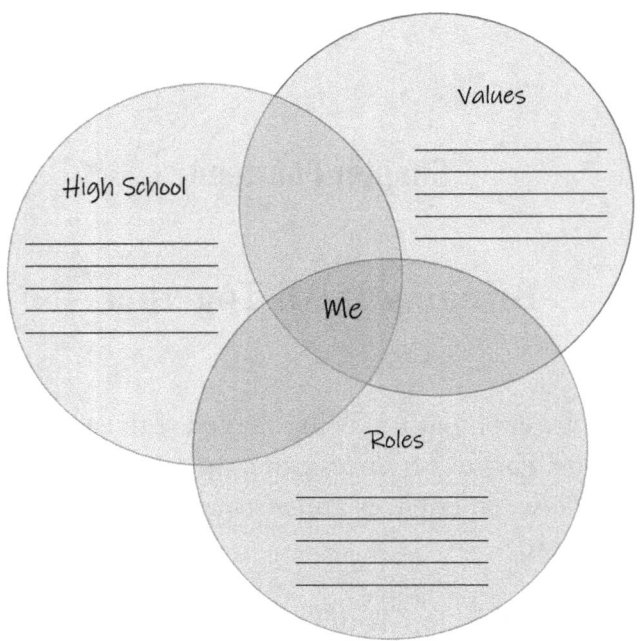

Step One: High School

Refer to the stories you wrote about high school in Chapter One's *Your Turn*. Look at what you wrote under the Reframe sections. Choose a phrase from these sections that really stands out for you. A phrase can come from one of your stories, things you would do differently, significant people in your life then, knowing what you know now, or advice you would give to current graduates. Write whatever speaks to you in the High School circle.

Step Two: Adversity

In one of the places where the circles overlap, label a section ADVERSITY. Write one lesson that adversity has taught you in the intersection.

Step Three: Messages and Your Inner Voice

If something stands out, write it somewhere on one of the three intersections. Messages we receive from teachers who come into our lives and the wisdom of our inner voice don't land in the same place for everyone, so place them where it feels right to you.

Step Four: Roles

Look at your mind map and what you discovered about a role you had during your impressionable years. Look at the list of roles and responsibilities and write down what stands out in the Roles circle.

Step Five: Your Values

Look at the list of your top five values and write them in your Values circle. Underline the value that is core to every other value on your list. Write a phrase or a few words about the connections between them.

Step Six: Change

Look back at your evolution as a parent: where you have come from, who you were, and how you have evolved into who you are today. In the intersection labeled CHANGE, write a few words or a phrase that describes one way you have changed.

Step Seven: Growth

Look at the thoughts you have put down on paper. How have you grown from who you were in the impressionable years? Write your observation in the Growth section.

Step Eight: Bringing It All Together

Refer to what you wrote in your Reframe sections for each *Your Turn* section and list them here.

High School: _____.
Number one insight you gained in High School:

_____.

Values: _____.
Number one insight from your Values:

_____.

Roles: _____.
Number one insight from your Roles in the world:

_____.

Adversity: _____.
Number one insight Adversity taught you:

_____.

Change: _____.
Number one insight from Change:

_____.

Growth: _____.
Number one insight from Growth:

_____.

Now, list your **Insights** from each section:
    1. **High School:** _____
    2. **Values:** _____
    3. **Roles:** _____
    4. **Adversity:** _____
    5. **Change:** _____
    6. **Growth:** _____

Your Turn: Connect the Dots

Create a sentence in the present tense incorporating your insights that represents how you make a difference. This is your light that you share with the world.

What makes me dance is: _____.

How will you share your light?
I will: _____.

Write your intention to share your light on a sticky note. Put this sticky note where you will see it every day to remind yourself of your greatness. Own your greatness, be the light in the world, and together we will make the world a better place.

I make the world a better place because: _____

This is my light I share with the world: _____

Sharing Your Light

Unravel you to discover your best parts and how you can make a remarkable difference in the world. I'm passing my light to you so you can share your light with someone else.

Share your journey. Inspire and be inspired by people who have moved through adversity and been transformed in the process. Share your light with people you meet and encourage them to do the same. Together, we can all light up the world. Trust your inner voice, stand up, speak up, and let's make the world a brighter, kinder, more joyful place.

Today and throughout history, women have been silenced. With all the turmoil and unrest in the world, it's time for women's voices to be heard. The world needs us. When I watch the news, it's clear men are still in power—many men, ruling with ego and a quest for control. Women are generally wired differently than men. It's not power and control we seek, it's harmony within our families and our communities and safety for our children, grandchildren, and people we love. The world can become a better place, one family, one friendship, workplace, community, or interaction at a time.

Every one of us can make a difference in the world. It starts with collectively connecting to what makes us dance and progresses toward inspiring others to do the same. Our inner light is passed from one person to the next, and the next, when we are making our personal mark in the world.

I have taken you through these steps to encourage you to peel back the layers of your life to discover what brought you to this place. Understanding where we have come from holds the key to knowing where we are going. Unravelling your past opens the door to discovering the more-evolved you. The world awaits your light. By letting go of old voices, reframing old experiences, embracing the wisdom they hold, and releasing the rest, you shine.

Now You're Talking

Join the community and stay connected by visiting www.unravelyou.com. You will meet like-minded people from around the world. The journey of self-reflection and self-discovery happens when the time is right and in the right timing. Together, the journey is less lonely and more empowering. You are not alone.

When you want to share your insights and have meaningful conversation with family and friends, you can purchase a game I created that encourages real conversation.

A fun and interactive board game that is perfect for all people ages eight to ninety-eight, *Now You're Talking* is a great addition to any family game night, party, or get-together with friends, and a must-have for anyone looking to bring people closer and understand one another better.

Gone are your evenings of boring, same-old, same-old small talk. From high school tales to family memories, this game will have you laughing, connecting, and learning about each other in ways you never thought possible.

The game is designed to bridge the generation gap. So parents, get ready to learn what your kids are *really* thinking. And kids, prepare to see your parents—or maybe even your grandparents—in a whole new light!

Now You're Talking is not your average board game. It's a powerful icebreaker in which strangers become friends and existing bonds are strengthened as you connect over shared experiences and heartfelt stories.

So, gather your family and friends around the table for a memorable evening and embark on an adventure that will leave you feeling connected, inspired, and entertained.

Let the conversations begin.

Now you're talking!

Order *Now You're Talking* today by visiting www.nowyouretalkinggame.com and become more connected, one conversation at a time.

People Are Talking About
Now You're Talking

Now You're Talking is a fun game to play as an icebreaker with people you don't know well, and great to play with friends you know well to find out things you didn't already know.

~ *Brent, age 28*

I played this game with a group of lifelong friends. It felt like an experience and game all in one! I left the night feeling so connected with everyone.

~ *Jess, age 25*

Now You're Talking challenges one to reflect on many aspects of their life. It brings out honesty and sometimes feelings and emotions that would otherwise never surface. You get to know some real surprises in others in a fun format that can change with every game.

~ *John, age 60*

This game is so fun and insightful! My childhood friends and I stayed up all night playing, sometimes laughing till we cried, and realizing we all had much more to our stories. . . . We loved it!

~ Nanc, age 64

Now You're Talking has the power to make an evening of forced conversation into an evening of stimulating conversation, connection, and best of all, laughter. It provides a platform to tell our stories and connect us though our adversities, our growth, and our personal quirks. I often find myself wishing I had *Now You're Talking* whenever I'm socializing, and the conversation feels dull. Sometimes, I simply want to spark engagement. *Now You're Talking* is so engaging I find myself hoping that people roll a low number, so the game doesn't have to end!

~ Ellereigh, age 31

I thought I knew everything there was to know about my wife, then we played *Now You're Talking*. In less than an hour, I had learned countless new things about her and why she is the way she is. It left me wanting to play more so I could learn and connect with her more.

~ Tom, age 35

You can play *Now You're Talking* a thousand times, and every time will be wildly different. Some games are filled with laughs, others may bring tears. No matter what, you'll be craving more.

~ Ella, age 32

I love playing *Now You're Talking* with my kids. I gain so much insight they don't normally share.

~ Leanne, age 45

When you play *Now You're Talking*, you get to know people you already know on a deeper level. You get to talk about things you wouldn't normally talk about.

~ Rach, age 36

When people play *Now You're Talking*, the answers they give are really funny, and you get to know who you're playing with really well. I think the game makes a lot of sense. It has a lot of pieces, but I was able to understand it really quickly. It's colourful and it's in my favourite colours. I really like it.

~ Mikayla, age 8

Now You're Talking gives the game participants an opportunity to get below the surface and really get to know one another. When we entertain, I am often the first to turn in. When we play *Now You're Talking*, I find new energy. This game sparks conversation that is both informative and stimulating. Because of this conversation, I stay up to the wee hours of the morning.

~ Bob, age 76

Acknowledgments

When I heard the voice within asking: *What makes you dance?* I told myself I would write a book one day. Those are simple words to say, difficult words to put into action. It has been the support of my faith and the encouragement of my family and friends, who have allowed me to turn my thoughts of writing a book into reality.

Although I was told writing a book would be transformational, it was difficult before the experience to imagine just how transformational it would be. Thank you to the community and the teams at Get Your Book Done and Seshat Press Publishing, who provided constant support, precise and thoughtful editing, and marketing expertise. Thank you to Carrie Jareed and Jean Merrill, who were both always there to help. I never felt alone in the process. A special thanks to Heather Taylor, my coach and editor, whose commitment to this project and her unwavering support helped me to put my thoughts on paper.

I would like to acknowledge my mom for being a constant source of inspiration. I have watched you battle adversity and with growing, evolving faith, emerge stronger. With courage and resilience, you have reinvented yourself and, by example, inspired me. You have always believed in me, have loved me unconditionally, and have provided reassurance along a sometimes-difficult journey.

Thank you to my brothers; your strength has also strengthened me. Thank you for always referring to me as the *Rose Between Two Thorns*.

Thank you, Beau, for your sense of humor and for believing in me. In the morning the alarm would sound at 4:45, a signal it was time to write. You would affectionately call me by some famous author's name. "Good luck _____!" I would hear as I walked down the hall, not knowing what words would land on paper. Writing days became your favourite days; it meant you had extra time to sleep. Upon my return you would anxiously ask, "How many words this morning?" Your humour and steadfast belief in my ability kept me moving forward.

I want to thank my daughters Reese, Kendra, Eve, and Mila. From the very beginning, you trusted me to tell your stories and encouraged me to be authentic and real. You have all had your struggles and you have all grown and thrived in adversity. Jokingly, you question who's my favourite, and I stay strong in my response. How could I possibly have a favourite when you are all so individual? Each one of you is making the world better in your own special way. RKEM, I admire all four of you; I have no favourites. I am thankful for your trust, your respect, and your forgiveness for all the mistakes I made as your mom. Thank you for your unconditional love.

Thank you to my blended family for accepting me wholeheartedly into your lives. You have all helped me to smooth out some rough edges along the way, and for that I'm very grateful.

Thank you, Nova. You have believed in me and have been my best friend for more than five decades. We have experienced many firsts together. After spending so much time together growing up, we see the world through the same lens. Although Canada separates us, you are always with me in my thoughts and in my heart.

Jade, thank you for always guiding me to see the world differently. We have had very different beginnings, growing up in opposite parts of the world. I appreciate how you challenge me to go deeper and to take off the blinders to see beyond my sometimes-limited beliefs.

Thank you to all you readers who have the courage to unravel the past to reflect and discover what makes you dance. Thank you for sharing your light in the world. The world needs you.

About the Author

A drienne lives in Vancouver, Canada, with Beau, her life and business partner. Together they own an executive recruitment and a digital marketing company.

Adrienne is part of a blended family of seven; two sons, five daughters, their partners, and six grandchildren.